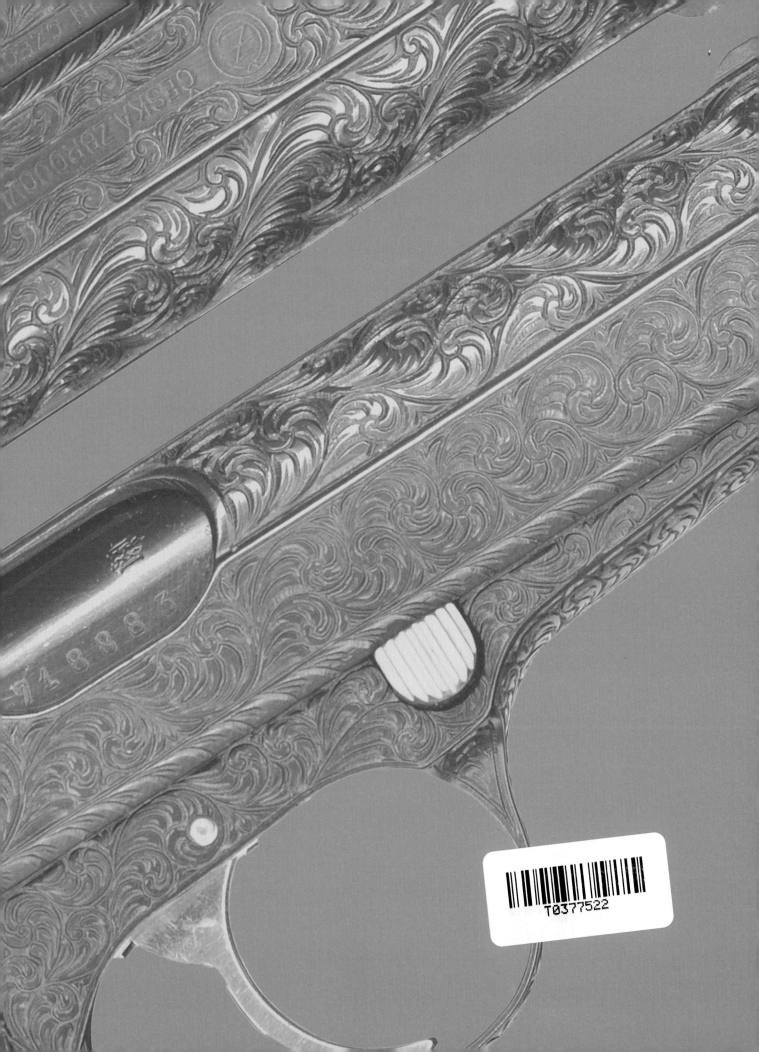

The ČZ Models 50 AND 70

Czech Cold War Police Pistols

James D. Brown

Schiffer Military History

4880 Lower Valley Road
Atglen, PA 19310

This book is not sponsored, endorsed, or otherwise affiliated with any of the companies whose products are represented herein, including those listed below. It is derived from the author's independent research.

A-Zoom is a trademark of Lyman Products Corporation, Middletown, CT, USA.
Bore Stores is a trademark of Galati International, Villa Ridge, MO, USA.
Break-Free CLP is a trademark of Break Free Inc., Santa Ana, CA, USA.
Brownells and **Oxpho-Blue** are trademarks of Brownells, Inc., Grinnell, IA, USA.
C.A.I. is a trademark of Century Arms International, Delray Beach, FL, USA.
Colt is a trademark of Colt's Manufacturing Co. LLC, Hartford, CT, USA.
Crown Bolt is a trademark of Crown Screw & Bolt Corporation, Indianapolis, IN, USA.
ČZ is a trademark of Česká zbrojovka a.s., Uherský Brod, Czech Republic.
Dremel is a trademark of Dremel US, a subsidiary of Robert Bosch GmbH, Gerlingen, Germany.
FN is a trademark of Fabrique Nationale Herstal, Herstal, Belgium.
Hogue and **Handall** are trademarks of Hogue Inc., Henderson, NV, USA.
Hornady is a trademark of Hornady Manufacturing Co., Grand Island, NE, USA.
Klinsky is a trademark of Klinsky & Co. s.r.o., Proseč, Czech Republic
Locktite is a trademark of Henkel AG & Co. KGaA, Düsseldorf, Germany.
Markall and **Paintstik** are trademarks of LA-CO Industries, Inc., Elk Grove Village, IL, USA.
Mauser is a trademark of Mauser Jagdwaffen GmbH, Isny im Allgäu, Germany.
Pro-Mag is a trademark of Pro-Mag Industries, Phoenix, AZ, USA.
Saf-T-Trainers is a trademark of Tactical Response, Camden, TN, USA.
Speer is a trademark of Speer Bullets, Lewiston, ID, USA.
Tipton is a trademark of American Outdoor Brands, Columbia, MO, USA.
Traditions is a trademark of Traditions Performance Firearms, Old Saybrook, CT, USA.
Triple K is a trademark of Triple K Manufacturing Co, a division of Krasne's Inc., San Diego, CA, USA.
Velcro is a trademark of FASTENation, Clifton, NJ, USA.
Walther is a trademark of Carl Walther GmbH Sportswaffen, Zella-Mehlis, Germany.
WD-40 is a trademark of the WD-40 Company, San Diego, CA, USA.

Other Schiffer books by the author
Cold War Pistols of Czechoslovakia, 978-0-7643-3354-5
Collector's Guide to Imperial Japanese Handguns, 1893–1945, 978-0-7643-2787-2

Other Schiffer books on related subjects
The MAT-49 Submachine Gun: And Preceding French Submachine Gun Designs, Including the MAS-35, Luc Guillou, 978-0-7643-6292-7
American Submachine Guns, 1919–1950: Thompson SMG, M3 "Grease Gun," Reising, UD M42, and Accessories, Luc Guillou, 978-0-7643-5484-7

Copyright © 2024 by James D. Brown

Library of Congress Control Number: 2023941125

All rights reserved. No part of this work may be reproduced or used in any form or by any means—graphic, electronic, or mechanical, including photocopying or information storage and retrieval systems—without written permission from the publisher.

The scanning, uploading, and distribution of this book or any part thereof via the Internet or any other means without the permission of the publisher is illegal and punishable by law. Please purchase only authorized editions and do not participate in or encourage the electronic piracy of copyrighted materials.

"Schiffer Military" and the arrow logo are trademarks of Schiffer Publishing, Ltd.

Designed by Christopher Bower
Cover design by Christopher Bower
Type set in Avenir

ISBN: 978-0-7643-6792-2
Printed in India

Published by Schiffer Publishing, Ltd.
4880 Lower Valley Road
Atglen, PA 19310
Phone: (610) 593-1777; Fax: (610) 593-2002
Email: Info@schifferbooks.com
Web: www.schifferbooks.com

For our complete selection of fine books on this and related subjects, please visit our website at www.schifferbooks.com. You may also write for a free catalog.

Schiffer Publishing's titles are available at special discounts for bulk purchases for sales promotions or premiums. Special editions, including personalized covers, corporate imprints, and excerpts, can be created in large quantities for special needs. For more information, contact the publisher.

We are always looking for people to write books on new and related subjects. If you have an idea for a book, please contact us at proposals@schifferbooks.com.

Contents

Preface		5
Acknowledgments		6
Chapter 1	Introduction and Description	8
Chapter 2	Production History	12
Chapter 3	Changes and Production Variations	40
Chapter 4	Marking Variations and Foreign Markings	56
Chapter 5	Anomalies, Oddities, and Unique Specimens	64
Chapter 6	Operational Features	88
Chapter 7	Disassembly and Assembly	94
Chapter 8	Holsters and Accessories	110
Chapter 9	Valuation	132
Chapter 10	Shooting and Maintenance	146
Appendix: Summary of Variants		154
Bibliography		159
Index		160

Preface

This book is an update and revision of chapter 2 from my book *Cold War Pistols of Czechoslovakia* (Schiffer, 2009). When that work was prepared, the chapter was based on records drawn from approximately eight hundred pistols, but there were significant data gaps, notably among vz. 50s from 1957 to 1966 and early 1970, and vz. 70s from 1974 to 1979 and 1982 to 1983. Some information was based on reports later found to be incomplete or inaccurate, resulting in erroneous conclusions and some variants being missed completely. Releases of surplus pistols since 2009 have expanded the number of records in the author's database to over 4,400 and his reference collection to eighty pistols, largely closing the 1957–66, early 1970, and 1974–79 data gaps, although data from 1960 and 1966 through mid-1967 remain sparse, and no pistols have been observed from 1957, 1963, or 1983. The author has benefited from more than a decade of additional study and has learned much more about these utilitarian pistols, but some questions remain.

Where possible, data have been verified both through Czech firearms literature and direct communication with firearms specialists in the Czech Republic, but specific information can be difficult to obtain due to language barriers and the simple fact that if one does not know what questions to ask, he is unlikely to learn the answers. Information on foreign arms sales is often considered sensitive and may be reserved for diplomatic reasons, so many questions on this subject remain unanswered. Although engineering drawings are required for all changes in factory tooling and, along with approval documents, are preserved in factory archives, without access to those records the information they contain is largely unavailable. As a result, the author has focused on the pistols themselves, examining specimens and recording serial numbers, acceptance dates, and specific features that define variants. This creates an unavoidably biased view of the subject because even though a great deal of information has been gathered on the "population" of Czech pistols in the US, data on those that have not reached our markets are missing except where it can be gleaned from Czech references. The terms "known" and "unknown," as used in this text, are in reference to the author's research; in most cases the missing information exists in the Czech Republic but has not been made available. Research will continue as new material appears, but it is time to share what has been learned with firearms enthusiasts and collectors.

Czech firearms authors, notably Jan Balcar, David Pazdera, and Jan Skramoušský, have done a commendable job of documenting the development, design, and production of Czech pistols from the birth of Czechoslovakia at the close of World War I until its peaceful dissolution at the end of 1992, as well as continuing progress in today's Czech Republic. Much of their work has focused on the inventors and industrialists who created, refined, and produced these weapons; the evolution of various designs; the role of government in corporate success; and the timing and extent of the resulting industrial output. However, little attention has been given to changes made during the production of any specific model—changes that define variations of interest to US collectors. This work examines a single design that originated as a post–World War II police pistol, became an important export item, and remained in commercial production through much of the Cold War era; it describes the array of modifications that were made to simplify production and enhance utility during its protracted service life, and offers information on disassembly, maintenance, repair, and valuation. Since the pistols were designed and built to metric system standards, metric units are used in their description; English units are used in describing most related items such as boxes and manuals.

Markings on most pistols used to illustrate the text have been filled with removable white Markall Paintstik for visibility. Digital photo editing has been employed to adjust lighting, remove backgrounds, and enhance clarity. Except where noted, photographs are by the author and subject matter is drawn from his collection.

• • •

Readers interested in asking questions or sharing data may contact the author by email at NambuKenjyu@hotmail.com

James D. Brown
November 2022

Acknowledgments

This work, like the volume that preceded it, is based both on the author's research and on information reported by other firearms collectors, dealers, and enthusiasts. For reasons of privacy and security, data sources are not recorded in the author's databases, which are simply consecutive lists of serial numbers with production dates and codes for variant-defining characteristics associated with individual pistols. Since this is a continuation of the research leading to the publication of *Cold War Pistols of Czechoslovakia*, names of contributors to that work are repeated here, with additions where appropriate. Many people have continued to submit data on new acquisitions or other material and their assistance is greatly appreciated. Clara C. Brown and Sue N. Brown assisted with the photography.

The internet auction sites GunAuction.com, GunBroker.com, GunsAmerica.com, and RockIslandAuction.com have been valuable sources of information. These sites list thousands of firearms, often providing photos showing details that are useful for research and in most cases offering an option to query the seller or auction house about details that are unclear or not visible. Without these sites it would have been impossible to build the databases that define variations and track the production history of the arms that are covered. Most of the author's reference collection was purchased through these sites.

Six individuals are due special thanks. In the US, Robert Lukes contributed a large amount of initial data that helped start this work. Alan J. Bell and H. Wayne Valentine made significant early contributions and have continued to provide data from specimens they encounter. Alan also provides information from periodic visits to the Czech Republic, including data and photos from museum collections there, and he gathered most of the manuals and sales brochures shown in chapter 8. In the Czech Republic, Jan Balcar and David Pazdera have provided information from their own work and data extracted from factory records. David provided copies of several of his books on Czech pistols and the ČZ company and both have assisted the author on questions regarding Czech language and firearms terminology. Vit Zemanek provided information as well as factory surplus grip panels used to restore some pistols.

The following individuals provided data or assistance:

Douglas Akers
Donald Althauser
Bill Amunrud
William Angelus
Terry Appling
Matt Astor
Chuck Atwell
Paul Bastean
Robert Beard
Bob Bollman
Wayne Brown
Ted Buckley
David Bunn
Shane Burkhardt
Chris Burnett
Bruce A. Bydal
Steve Carpenter
Jim Cate
Frank Ceely
Mike Cipisek
Jules Cody
David Cook
Dale Crabtree
Barry S. Craig
Colin Doane
Mark J. Donahue
Frank Ellenbecker
Rick Eplin
Ken Evans
Jack Farrar
Roger Fee
Dick Fonnet
Steve Fox
Mitch France
Andy Galante
Al Gerth
W. E. Goethe

Marcel Grodwohl
John Hardin
Tim Hawkins
Tom Heller
Ed Helmeister
Patrick Hibbits
Robert E. Hogan
Brandon Hose
Denver Hough
Ron Janosek
Cecil Roy Jergensen
Bob Jones
Chris Jowers
Charlie Justmann
Eric Keifer
Al Kellis
Thompson Knox Sr.
Ken Koch
Tom Kyriakiks
Dan Larkin
R. Douglas Lawrence
Dee Lazarus
Robert Lieder
Dan Liggett
Jack Love
Fred Ludowikowski
Mark Mann
John A. Masseo
Art May
Ellis McCurdy
Connell Miller
William L. Morris
Marv Nieman
Kevin Null
Bryan Oaldon
Robert O'Connor
Greg Olsen

Leonid V. Orlov
Steve Oswald
Kenneth Pennington
Paul A. Phillip
Alice Poluchova
Joe Price
Barry A. Pringle
Tim Reynolds
Matt Rice
Ed Roane
Donald F. Rogers
Charlie Romero
John Rupp
Brian Scales
Allen Schoop
Richard Scott
Juerg Siegenthaler
David L. Smith
John Stork
Robert Sweet
Chris Teeter
Donald G. Thomas
Lawrence Tice
George Tich
Roger Tremblay
Lyle Truax
Jimmy Van Coutren
Tim Vaugn
Mark Wagner
Mitchell Warren
Doug Wight
Walter H. Williams
Carl H. Wittevrongel
Carl Wolter
Mark J. Yavno

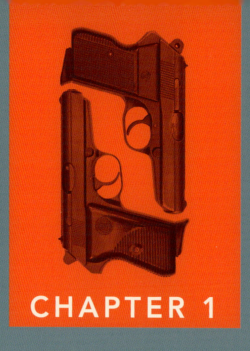

CHAPTER 1

Introduction and Description

In 1945, Czechoslovakia emerged from World War II German occupation with an assortment of military and police pistols, many of them war-worn or obsolete. Production of the 7.65 mm ČZ Model 27 was maintained, both to generate revenue and to keep factory workers employed, but a more modern police pistol was desired. The Czechs admired the highly successful Walther PP but wanted a less expensive weapon free from German licensing. They had lived under a parliamentary democracy from the founding of Czechoslovakia in 1918 until the 1938 German invasion, but seven years of brutal Nazi rule left them hostile toward their former masters. The provisional postwar government was plagued by retaliation against Bohemian Germans and the need to resettle them in Germany, tension between Czechs and Slovaks, and strife between Social Democrats and Communists over control of key government ministries. The Communists gained control of the Ministry of the Interior and in February 1948 led a coup that did not immediately affect the development of Czech arms, but the socialist government it produced nationalized businesses and industries under state control. Česká zbrjovka a. s. (*akclová společnost*, "joint stock company") was transformed from a privately owned corporation managed for profit to Česká zbrojovka n. p. (*národní podnik*, "national enterprise"), a government entity managed for the benefit of the state and the Communist Party. Over the next four decades, this would profoundly influence not only the production of Czech police pistols but the development and production of military and commercial firearms as well.

The brothers Jan and Jaroslav Kratochvíl began designing both a 7.65 mm police pistol and a 9 mm army pistol (later modified to 7.62 × 25 mm to meet Soviet demands) in 1947, employing similar firing mechanisms in both models, and the resulting police pistol was adopted in 1950 as the *vzor* (model) 50. Over the next thirty-three years its manufacture was terminated, relocated, restarted, suspended, and relocated again; numerous minor changes were adopted and it was eventually given a cosmetic upgrade and renamed *vzor* 70. In the US, vz. 50s are classified as "curios and relics" while vz. 70s were not, prior to 2020, an important legal distinction for licensed collectors; on the basis of their acceptance dates, as vz. 70s reach the age of fifty years they also become curios and relics. There are minor weight and dimensional differences between the two models but most changes occurred during the production of the vz. 50, not in the model change to vz. 70. Both models share the same basic design and in this text the term "vz. 50-70" is used as a joint reference.

Introduction and Description

1950 commercial vz. 50 serial number 663992 in factory new condition

Chapter 1

1971 vz. 70 serial number D94854. This pistol's markings were not highlighted in order to present it in unaltered factory-new condition.

The vz. 50-70 is an unlocked breech, blowback-operated semiautomatic pistol chambered for the 7.65 × 17 mm Browning cartridge (.32 ACP); it was produced experimentally in 9 mm Browning Short (.380 ACP), the only known example being 1965 serial number B66004 (Skramoušský and Badalík 1996, 223). Consideration was given to adapting it to 9 mm Makarov and a 7.65 mm compact prototype was developed, but neither of these ideas was advanced into production and in 1983 production of the vz. 70 was terminated in favor of the newly developed ČZ 83. In addition to serving the Czech police, vz. 50-70s were sold commercially and widely exported. They are compact, sturdy pistols, 166 mm (6.5") long and 121 mm (4.7") high including the magazine finger rest, with a 96 mm (3.8") barrel having six-groove rifling with a right-hand twist of one turn in 12". Listed weight is 1.5 lbs. unloaded (710 g for the vz. 50 and 670 g for the vz. 70), although the vz. 50's weight varied over time due to the effects of design changes. Magazine capacity is eight cartridges, although this is sometimes misjudged due to the provision of only seven cartridge-counter holes. The trigger mechanism allows double-action firing of the first shot, while subsequent shots are single action. The safety incorporates a decocking mechanism and firing-pin travel is controlled by a positive locking device that prevents discharge unless the trigger is pulled fully. The extractor engages a cartridge indicator that protrudes 1 mm from the left rear of the slide when the chamber is loaded, allowing verification of readiness by touch. The magazine catch is located at the top front of the left grip panel, a disassembly button is mounted on the receiver above the right front of the trigger guard, and the magazine catch, safety lever, and cartridge indicator all are within the normal arc of movement of a right-handed adult shooter's thumb.

The grip frame is open on the right side (an idea borrowed from Frantisek Dušek's 6.35 mm DUO pistol), incorporating the magazine well and firing-mechanism recesses into the receiver forging to simplify machining. The grip frame is enclosed at the bottom by a bridge on the left and the right grip panel encloses the magazine well on the opposite side, supporting the frame. A sideplate encloses the firing mechanism on the right, retained by a flange at the front and the hammer pivot nut at the rear. The sights are fixed, but the rear is drift adjustable for windage; the front blade is tapered, with a 1 mm width at its top, while the rear notch is U shaped and 2 mm wide.

The Kratchvils' pistol mimics the Walther PP in size and weight and shares its major features, arguably in a more convenient format for the shooter and at a substantially lower cost. It is often erroneously described as a Walther copy or clone by those who have not studied it in detail, but it should more properly be called a Walther substitute. While less familiar to many firearms enthusiasts than its German counterpart, the vz. 50-70 was an advance in Czech pistol technology that provided export revenue and served domestic police forces for half a century. Although it is often viewed as a somewhat drab, ordinary pistol, readers will find that it is surprisingly complex and interesting.

Since Czechoslovakia was never involved in a "hot" war during the service life of the vz. 50-70, these pistols lack the glamour that is often associated with war trophies. However, vz. 50-70s played roles in many clandestine operations during the Cold War and while designed for police use, they saw military service in the American war in Vietnam, the Middle Eastern conflicts that broke out repeatedly between Israel and its neighbors during the second half of the twentieth century and the early decades of the twenty-first, and many less well-known engagements throughout the world. They were purchased by military and police agencies in Africa, Asia, Central and South America, and Europe; they were exported for commercial sale in the US in the 1950s; and large numbers of them were later imported by US surplus arms dealers. While many of them have been replaced by more-modern and more-powerful arms, vz. 50-70s continue to serve both public and private defense needs today. For the collector, they represent a surprising level of complexity; more than forty production and marking variations have been documented, and the Czech practice of dating firearms acceptance adds another layer of interest with thirty different production dates, some of them quite rare. There are a number of unusual errors and oddities, a possible "mystery" variant suggested by promotional illustrations for which specimens have not been documented, a compact version produced as a prototype, and a little-known vz. 69. There was also a considerable variety of holsters, accessories, manuals, and promotional material produced for them. They offer a unique niche for those who appreciate variations and nuances but cannot afford to invest in more-expensive historic arms. For those who are not specific collectors of Czech arms and own only one or two of these pistols, it may be interesting to know where their specimens fit into the vz. 50-70 universe.

It is worth noting that the Yugoslav Zastava Arms Company introduced a 7.65 mm Browning pistol in 1970, the Crvena Zastava, which is also referred to as the CZ 70, sometimes erroneously linking it to Czechoslovakia. It is actually a scaled-down, unlocked breech version of the Soviet TT33, which Yugoslavia adopted as their M-57, and has no relationship with the Czech vz. 70 other than its similar nomenclature.

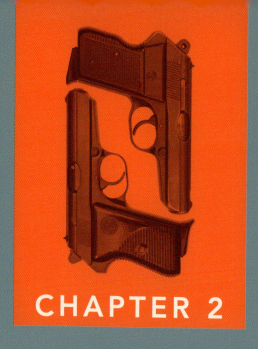

CHAPTER 2

Production History

Prototype ČZ 006, from an artist's drawing in the first instruction manual

The Kratochvíl brothers' final prototype for the new police pistol, number ČZ 006, was completed in 1948 and after extensive trials the design was adopted in 1950. Manufacture of the vz. 50 began at the ČZ factory in Strakonicé, South Bohemia, early that year with a contract to produce 64,000 pistols for the Ministry of the Interior's National Security Corps and an estimated five hundred for the Ministry of Justice; a portion of the factory output was designated for commercial export sales through the Ministry of Foreign Trade's Merkuria Corporation, although some of the commercial production was evidently delivered to Czech municipal police departments. The production start-up date was probably in early February and an estimated 46,819 pistols were accepted that year. For the Czechs the pistol was a significant evolution in design, with improved safety features, a dual-mode firing mechanism, and an innovative hold-open device; it was also modestly priced in comparison to similar-sized weapons from Colt, FN, Mauser, and Walther. Early international orders included 7,000 pistols for the Soviet Union and 102 for Abyssinia (modern Ethiopia).

Pistols produced for the National Security Corps, Sbor národní bezpečností, are marked on the front grip strap with the letters *NB* followed by the two-digit acceptance date, 50, 51, or 52. Those allocated to the Ministry of Justice (Ministerstvo spravedlností) were produced only in 1950 and are marked "MS 50" on the front grip strap; they are scarce and most known specimens are from the 675000–678000 serial blocks. Approximately 24,300 Strakonicé vz. 50s were produced for commercial sale and are scattered randomly among the government contract pistols; the method of allocating production to government and commercial use is not known. Due to Communist-era restrictions on civilian firearms ownership commercial vz. 50s were not sold domestically, although a few may have been presented to high-ranking Communist Party officials. Early

Production History

Government contract vz. 50 MS and NB front grip strap markings

commercial vz. 50s carry no grip strap markings but are identified by a commercial "Lion-N" proof (🦁) stamped above (or in some very early pistols, forward of) the acceptance date on the left side of the slide, just forward of the gripping grooves. The Czech army did not use vz. 50s, although a small number of vz. 70s were delivered to the Ministry of Defense in 1979; none of these pistols have been documented and the author has been unable to determine whether they carried military markings.

Both government contract and commercial vz. 50s produced at Strakonicé carry proof marks over the chamber, visible through the ejection port when the slide is in battery. On commercial pistols the 🦁 proof is clearly stamped, but on early government contract pistols it is usually shallow and can be difficult to identify. Czech proofing law was changed in 1950 to allow arms factories to proof weapons internally rather than submitting them to an independent proofing house, applying a Ⓣ mark (*tormentační*) rather than the commercial 🦁 although its use did not become established at Strakonicé until 1951 at about serial number 704000. *Tormentační* marks are normally 4.5 mm in diameter, but a 2.5 mm die was used on some early pistols and its impressions may be light and difficult to see without magnification. Although used only on government firearms, the Ⓣ mark represents factory rather than government authority.

Serialization of the vz. 50 began at number 650001 (Skramoušský and Badalík 1996, 220), sequential to the ČZ Model 27 pistol, although there is a gap—evidently intentional—of about 25,000 numbers between the highest known ČZ 27 serial and the lowest vz. 50. (In 2009, the author reported two vz. 50 serial numbers below 650001 from US collections, but the weight of additional data demonstrates that these were either mistakes in reading or transposing numerals or factory errors.) Serial numbering was done by hand, and while efforts were made to maintain an orderly appearance, especially during the early production period, there were times when the workmanship was downright sloppy. (There is evidence that the first two serial digits were applied with a single die, at least during most of the Strakonicé production period; this can be seen in the alignment and spacing of those numerals compared to the rest of the serial number.) To avoid a production bottleneck multiple serial-numbering stations worked in parallel, using blocks of numbers that were probably assigned in the form of checkoff cards that were collected and replaced when completed; this would

Lightly stamped commercial proof used on early government contract vz. 50s

Normal *tormentační* proof used on Strakonicé vz. 50s

Early small *tormentační* proof

Strakonicé commercial vz. 50s are proofed and dated on the left side of the slide forward of the gripping grooves.

Czech Cold War Police Pistols

Chapter 2

Serial number 650564 was produced during the first month of operation at Strakonicé for commercial sale and saw extensive service before being imported by C.A.I. in the 1990s.

Serial number 652791 was produced in 1950 for the National Security Corps.

Production History

Serial number 675613 was produced in 1950 for the Ministry of Justice.

Excerpt from a 1950s magazine ad by a California firearms dealer for the "CZ New Model .006." The dealer evidently mistook the prototype serial number for the model number. *Courtesy of Roger Tremblay*

Czech Cold War Police Pistols 15

Chapter 2

Consecutive serial numbers do not imply similar histories. NB 50–marked number 664019 was produced for the Ministry of the Interior in May 1950, evidently saw little service use, was declared surplus and imported by Intrac Arms International of Knoxville, Tennessee, in the first few years of the 2000s, and was purchased by a collector in Rockingham, North Carolina, who sold it to the author in 2008. Number 664020 was produced for commercial sale at the same time; was imported by Thalson Co. of San Francisco, California, later that year; and spent most of the next half century in a storage cabinet or drawer; it was purchased from the original owner's heir by a dealer in Carson City, Nevada, who sold it to the author in 2004. Both remain in nearly immaculate condition after more than seventy years.

prevent duplication, avoid confusion during breaks and shift changes, and provide management with a means of monitoring production in progress. It contributed to the "overlapping" phenomenon discussed below and explains why it is evident even in carefully planned changes such as the new model introduction in 1970, since each numbering station would have executed the change at a different point in the serial sequence. Although the letter serial prefixes B, C, D, and J which were used from 1957 to 1972 were applied at the same time as the serial number, the star and triangle serial prefixes used in 1977–83 were evidently added when the pistols were proofed and accepted.

The "overlapping" of serial numbers, dates, and changes that is evident in production tables is the result of a common practice in firearms manufacturing. Individual parts were collected in bins or other receptacles as they came off the machinery; those requiring fitting (in this case receivers, sideplates, and slides) were drawn from the bins and matched, serial-numbered, and placed in assembly trays. The trays were gathered in racks on pallets or wheeled carts which were moved to the assembly area, where they were processed through several parallel lines, emerging in random order; completed pistols were inspected, proofed, and dated following acceptance. The randomization produced by this process prevents serial numbers and dates from being synchronized; pistols have been observed that are far out of sequence, perhaps as a result of temporary pauses in one or more assembly lines, racks of trays backing up in storage and being processed out of order, or initial rejection of pistols followed by adjustment and resubmission for acceptance. When a change such as a new style of hammer was introduced, as long as the parts were compatible mixing of new- and old-style parts occurred until the supply of old parts was exhausted; this, coupled with random assembly order, resulted in overlapping of serial numbers and production changes. (As an example of randomization, test target dates for six known vz. 70s tested in February 1971 are D93403, 2/5; D95722 and D95731, 2/12; D95333 and D95546, 2/16; and D94854, 2/17.)

After an impressive start in 1950 production slowed in 1951, probably as a result of political turmoil; there were widespread purges, some people vanished while others were publicly shamed or executed, and more than 120,000 were arrested, often on unspecified charges, and sent to

Table 2-1	Strakonicé vz. 50 Production	
Year	Observed serial range	Estimated total
1950	650036–704512	46,819
1951	670617–720514	19,055
1952	706011–739535	22,949
		88,823

forced-labor camps. The factory output accelerated somewhat in 1952, but production was terminated after completion of the government contract in order to focus resources on military needs for the vz. 52 army pistol. Like the start-up date, the production termination date has not been published, but the army inspector began accepting vz. 52s in December so vz. 50 production probably ended in September or early October to allow the new tooling to be installed and adjusted. The highest observed vz. 50 serial number is NB 52–marked 739535; annual production estimates are summarized in table 2-1. Strakonicé factory records place the total number of pistols produced at 88,823, although subtracting the serialization starting point, 650001, from the highest observed serial number yields a total of 89,534. These figures are actually not incompatible, since some pistols undoubtedly failed to pass inspection and were not counted as being produced; the difference represents a rejection rate of 0.8 percent, a reasonable figure for that time period. In 1954 the Strakonicé factory was ordered to terminate all arms manufacturing and shift to civilian products, although the order was not executed until the army pistol contract was completed in March 1955. The company name was changed from Česká zbrjovka (Czech Armory) to Český závody motocyklové (Czech Motorcycle Works), or ČZM; this political decision effectively squandered the knowledge and experience of the trained firearms staff at Strakonicé.

By 1956 the Czechs realized that terminating vz. 50 production had been a mistake; commercial pistol sales had been an important source of revenue and the country was in a business recession and needed to boost export trade (Pazdera 2013). Discussions were held in Prague and a decision was reached to restart vz. 50 production at Zavod Přesné Strojírenství (Precision Engineering Co., or ZPS UB),

Chapter 2

Serial number 688094 was produced in 1951 for commercial export sale.

Serial number 707141 was produced in 1951 for the National Security Corps.

Production History

Serial number 728834 was produced in 1952 for commercial export sale.

Serial number 739260 was among the last Strakonicé vz. 50s produced in 1952 for the National Security Corps.

Chapter 2

Serial number B12078 was produced at ZUB in 1958; smooth trigger, type 1 magazine.

Serial number B24998 was produced at ZUB in 1959; grooved trigger, type 1 magazine.

the ČZ branch factory at Uherský Brod, Moravia, later known as Zavod Uherský Brod, or ZUB as used in this text. (After the reestablishment of democratic government in 1990, the company was reorganized as today's ČZUB.) Engineering drawings and some tooling were transferred to the new location, as well as authorization to use the encircled ČZ trademark, and production was restarted there in late 1957; plans called for production of 2,000 pistols that year with an annual output of 10,000 thereafter. From the beginning, however, there were problems. Critical machinery that had been promised could not be delivered because it had already been transferred and put to use elsewhere, starting a legal fight between ČZM and ZUB that delayed the start-up and nearly ended the project before it began. Receiver forgings had to be produced by Moravské kovárny (Moravian Smitheries) in Jihlava, plastic grip panels and magazine finger rests were supplied by Lisovny nových hmot (New Materials Pressing Works) in Chuchelná, and magazine springs were made by ČZM in Strakonicé. Factory space was already crowded with target pistol and military rifle production and there was no room for the new machinery when it finally arrived. A pistol workshop was set up in a former furniture repair company building behind the railway station, but there were difficulties with parts for the firing mechanism; magazines were also a serious problem and required hand-fitting to individual pistols until fabrication was perfected in 1958. Thirty-two pistols had been assembled for testing and evaluation by September 27, 1957, but some of them did not function properly and required adjustment. The workshop completed 510 pistols that year and in 1958 production surpassed targets, but problems continued to plague the operation. After 1958 production lagged behind targets and in 1963, quality control issues forced operations to be suspended; a new manufacturing hall was built at ZUB, the equipment and tooling were moved into it, and production was restarted in 1964 (Pazdera 2013).

During the 1963 operational suspension, pistols were unavailable for export sales and a decision was made to withdraw cases of government-owned vz. 50s previously produced at Strakonicé from storage, modify them for target use, and offer them on the export market as "Sport" pistols. The conversions were done by the Lovena workshop (David Pazdera, personal communication), which also produced air- and CO_2-powered target pistols, and known specimens carry commercial proofs and "63" dates on the left side of the slide forward of the gripping grooves, as was done with commercial pistols produced at Strakonicé; the original grip strap property markings were retained. The number of pistols converted has not been published, but they are well known to Czech arms enthusiasts and are fairly widely distributed in European countries that allow private ownership of firearms; they are covered in more detail in chapter 5.

When production of the vz. 50 was restarted at ZUB in 1957 the serialization system was revised; the consecutive six-digit numbers employed at Strakonicé were replaced by five-digit numbers preceded by a letter prefix. The first series was designated B and began with serial number 10001; Czech 6.35 mm vz. 45 and Z pistols were also given B serial prefixes when their production was transferred to ZUB, so the prefix was evidently intended to indicate the new production facility and was only later viewed as an alphabetical series designator that could be changed to prevent serial numbers from exceeding five digits.

ZUB applied a commercial proof on the left rear of the slide and a second proof on the upper left front of the trigger guard.

Chapter 2

Serial number B31710 was produced at ZUB in 1960; grooved trigger, type 1 magazine.

Serial number B42327 was produced at ZUB in 1962, shortly before the 1963 operational suspension: grooved trigger, type 1 magazine.

Production History

Serial number B62964 was produced in 1964; "forged" slide, type 2 magazine.

Serial number B69414 was produced at ZUB in 1965; machined slide, type 2 magazine (correct but not original to this pistol). Its mechanical problems are discussed in chapter 6.

Czech Cold War Police Pistols

Chapter 2

All ZUB vz. 50s carry commercial markings, with the ⊠ proof and acceptance date stamped on the left side of the slide to the rear of the cartridge indicator and another ⊠ proof stamped on the left side of the receiver at the upper front of the trigger guard. The supply of pistols for the National Security Corps apparently remained adequate and pistols for Czech municipal police were drawn from the normal production stream during this period and carry no special markings.

Most of the ZUB vz. 50s were consigned to the Merkuria Corporation for export sale. Data from pistols produced at ZUB during the early years are somewhat sparse because trade with the US was very limited and international sales were widely dispersed, making pistols involved in them difficult to locate and study. Observations from 1960 are almost nonexistent, while those from 1965 through mid-1967 are scarce. No annual production totals have been published for 1964 through 1966 but a total of about 30,550 pistols were produced during those years, an estimated 18,800 in 1964, 9,944 in 1965, and 1,529 in 1966. (There was probably a backlog of serialized receiver-slide sets on hand when production was suspended in 1963, explaining the surge in output following the restart in 1964. However, the observed 1964 serial range suggests a fairly high rejection rate, reflecting the problems that led to the 1963 suspension; the subsequent output decline in 1966 has not been explained.)

In 1967, production accelerated considerably and several design changes were implemented. A change in the magazine body was adopted early in the year but overlapping was extensive, continuing at least until June. Between late April and June, the original solid hammer was replaced with a ring type; serial number B99999 was reached in June (Skramoušský and Badalík 1996, 222) and was followed by the C series, beginning with serial number 00001. In July, the length of the gripping area on the slide was extended from 22 mm to 32 mm, the number of grooves was increased from fifteen to twenty-one, and the smooth sighting rib on the top of the slide was embossed in a wave pattern to eliminate glare. In late July or early August, the slide-gripping grooves were enlarged and their number reduced to sixteen, retaining the 32 mm gripping length, and a few weeks later a magazine-retaining spring was added to the grip frame to prevent magazines from falling free when released and becoming damaged or lost.

The calendar change from 1967 to 1968 occurred at about serial number C21000, the change from 1968 to 1969 was at about serial number C64000, with considerable overlapping, and the C series was completed close to the end of 1969; a change in the disassembly button was also made at that time. Data from this period are sparse, with only nine records from the C95000–D05000 serial range, but one 1970-dated C-series pistol (C95444) and one 1969-dated D-series pistol (D03897) are known, demonstrating that production of both series overlapped the 1969–70 calendar change. Another minor change in the hammer design occurred in early 1970. Annual production totals and observed serial number ranges for ZUB vz. 50s are provided in table 2-2 (Pazdera and Skramoušský 2006, 91–93). On the basis of serial numbers, the total number of ZUB vz. 50s produced was approximately 268,800; this figure makes no allowance for pistols failing to pass inspection, but it is assumed that quality control measures adopted following the 1964 relocation were effective in reducing defects in later pistols. Adding this figure to the 88,823 vz. 50s produced at Strakonice yields a grand total of 357,623 vz. 50s, although this should be considered an estimate due to the assumptions involved.

Production of the vz. 50 at ZUB continued until late August 1970. By the end of 1967, the cumulative effects of production changes had altered the pistols'

Table 2-2	ZUB vz. 50 Production	
Year	**Observed serial range**	**Reported total**
1957	B10001	510
1958	B10347–B25453	12,000
1959	B24552–B31903	8,000
1960	B31710–B323xx	2,001
1961	B33045–B36157	4,200
1962	B37260–B43716	7,077
1963		171
1964	B44161–B64320	18,800 est.
1965	B64262–B74344	9,944 est.
1966	B75985–B77514	1,529 est.
1967	B78260–C21421	43,000
1968	C20716–C69946	43,093
1969	C62049–D03897	40,202
1970	C95444–D78954	78,000 est.
		268,800

Production History

Serial number B85506 was produced in April 1967; smooth "forged" slide rib, solid hammer, type 3 magazine.

Serial number B99705 was produced in June 1967; smooth "forged" slide rib, ring hammer, fifteen slide grooves, type 3 magazine (correct but not original to this pistol).

Czech Cold War Police Pistols

Chapter 2

Serial number C02239 was produced in July or August 1967; embossed wave pattern slide rib, ring hammer, twenty-one slide grooves, type 3 magazine.

Serial number C05333 was produced in September 1967; impressed pattern slide rib, ring hammer, sixteen slide grooves, type 3 magazine.

Production History

Serial number C24471 was produced in 1968.

Serial number C91882 was produced in 1969; large-hole ring hammer, grooved disassembly button.

Czech Cold War Police Pistols

Chapter 2

Serial number D77630 was produced in 1970; small-hole ring hammer, checkered disassembly button.

appearance and handling characteristics, new holsters were being developed (some successful and some not), and a new commercial box was on the drawing board. A decision was made to upgrade the pistol cosmetically and offer it as a new model, although its mechanical design remained unchanged, but political turmoil surrounding General Secretary Alexander Dubček, the 1968 Prague Spring movement, and the subsequent Soviet invasion of Czechoslovakia on the night of August 20–21 to suppress democratic reforms probably interrupted the process. Dubček was forced to sign a treaty revoking the reforms and instituting a policy of "normalization" under socialist rule, but the seeds of dissent had found fertile ground. In spite of the repression of democracy, the Czechs wanted increased contact and trade with the West and modernizing the vz. 50 for increased export sales was a step in that direction. Amid this turmoil, a prototype was developed as the vz. 69 (David Pazdera, personal communication), and a number of these pistols were produced for testing and evaluation; existing specimens are apparently retained in the Czech Republic. Acceptance of the new model was delayed until 1970 and production of the vz. 70 began on August 20 of that year (Pazdera 2015, 175) at approximately serial number D78800. (This number was derived from the best available data in 2009; subsequent observations demonstrate a slightly lower starting point, but since the two models overlapped and the number is used primarily to distribute production between them it is pointless to continually revise it.)

During the period when the vz. 69 was being developed, plans were also underway to produce a smaller Kompaktní (compact) version of the pistol. Viskočíl and Frenzl (1996) provide photos of one of these pistols with vz. 50 markings on the cover and page 48 but offer no further details on its characteristics and development, simply labeling it a vz. 50. Pazdera (2015, 177) covers it in a sidebar, indicating that it was reconsidered in 1975 and proposed for

Production History

adoption as the vz. 80, but the idea was eventually shelved. The pistol had a shortened receiver fore end, slide, barrel, and recoil spring; a revised disassembly button mounted on the inside of the trigger guard similar to the type used on the Sauer model 38H; and a revised safety lever of the same type used on the vz. 69, but it retained the standard grip frame size and magazine. Photos of this pistol are presented in chapter 5.

The transition between the vz. 50 and vz. 70 is rather interesting, since there was no clean break between the two models and considerable overlapping occurred. Available serial number data are summarized in table 2-3, but the gaps leave much room for speculation about the way the process unfolded. On the basis of average production rates at the time, the transition lasted about three days and involved approximately a thousand pistols, most if not all from the D78000 serial block. The four lowest-known vz. 70s, serial numbers D78266, D78308, D78427, and D78512, consist of vz. 50 receivers fitted with matching-numbered vz. 70 slides, grip panels, and magazines, creating a transitional variant for which numbers are difficult to estimate. To date, no vz. 70 receivers fitted with vz. 50 slides and furniture have been identified, suggesting that the transitional variant was the result of an oversupply of vz. 50 receivers rather than a general mixing of parts from both models, but as additional specimens appear there may be surprising revelations.

Only three production changes were applied to the vz. 70 after the transition period, all of them internal, so the pistol's appearance remained unchanged for the remainder of production. The calendar change from 1970 to 1971 occurred at approximately serial number D86000 and the D series was completed in February 1971. For unknown reasons, the alphabetical order of serial prefixes was changed at that time and the D series was followed by the J series, which was completed in 1972. Serial number overlapping was much more extensive than usual during 1971–72, beginning at about serial number J60500 and extending over a range of more than 40,000 numbers. The reason for this was evidently a surge in production following the introduction of the new model, since 1971 had the highest level of production in the pistols' history. The quantities of serial-numbering stations and assembly lines were

Table 2-3	Vz. 50-70 Serial Number Overlap	
Vz. 50		**Vz. 70**
D77680		
D77734		
D77847		
D78055		
D78187		
		D78266
		D78308
D78340		
		D78427
		D78512
D78696		
		D78822
D78876		
		D78941
D78954		
		D79097
		D79385
		D79452
		D79499
		D79712
		D79846

evidently increased and backlogs probably developed, exacerbating the conditions that prevented pistols from being completed in sequential order. When the J series was completed in 1972, the use of serial prefixes was discontinued; number J99999 was followed by 100000 and consecutive six-digit numbering continued from that point until the end of production in 1983. Serial number 200000 was reached in late 1974, 300000 in 1976, 400000 in 1977, and 500000 in early 1979.

Czech Cold War Police Pistols

Chapter 2

"Transitional" vz. 70 serial number D78308 was produced in September 1970; note the vz. 50 receiver contours around the trigger guard and the space between the gripping grooves and the rear of the right side of the slide, which was increased in the vz. 70 to make room for the ČZ logo at the rear on the left side.

Production History

Serial number D98628 was produced in February 1971.

Serial number J08375 was produced in April 1971.

Czech Cold War Police Pistols

Chapter 2

After completion of the J series, the serial prefix was dropped and consecutive serialization continued using six-digit numbers; 100032 was produced in 1972.

Serial number 160007 was produced in 1973.

Production History

Serial number 196811 was produced in 1974.

Serial number 212443 was produced in 1975.

Czech Cold War Police Pistols

Chapter 2

Serial number 277218 was produced in 1976; original-type hold-open catch, type 4 magazine.

Serial number 402854 was produced in 1977; revised hold-open catch, type 5 magazine.

34   The ČZ Models 50 and 70

Production History

Serial number 467782 was produced in 1978 and issued to the Ostrava Municipal Police.

Serial number 516159 was produced in 1979.

Czech Cold War Police Pistols

Chapter 2

Star serial prefix number
☆353659, produced in 1977

Table 2-4	ZUB vz. 70 Production	
Year	Observed serial range	Reported total
1970	D78266–DD86787	7,200*
1971	D85170–101899	85,000
1972	J12672–135627	68,640
1973	135390–170565	30,806
1974	164092–203873	28,430
1975	199587–276818	60,050
1976	263887–325726	70,440
1977	278299–431871	77,970
1978	421202–487754	66,816
1979	512498–626832	79,837
1980	☆588590–△654720	76,287
1981	△650819–△723894	66,509
1982	660400–△723524	8,445
1983	—	425
		726,853

* Estimated from observations

By 1975 the Ministry of the Interior (Ministerstvo Vnitro, or MV) was again in need of pistols for its National Security Corps and in 1976 the use of a five-pointed-star serial prefix was authorized for marking vz. 70s for MV use. All but 2,340 pistols produced that year were consigned to the Merkuria Corporation for export sale and in 1977 all but three hundred pistols were exported, but in 1978 the cumulative MV demand was finally met and only 13,667 vz. 70s were exported, with the balance reserved for domestic use (Pazdera and Skramoušský 2006, 141). Not all of the domestic production went to the MV, since specimens dated both 77 and 78 in the author's collection are known to have come from the Ostrava Municipal Police and are not star-marked. In 1979, twenty vz. 70s were delivered to the Ministerstvo národní obrany (Ministry of Defense), probably for internal security use; this is the only known instance of vz. 50-70s being delivered to Czech military forces. Some pistols continued to be provided to the MV through 1980, bringing the total to over 65,000, but star-prefix vz. 70s remain scarce in the US with only sixteen recorded in the author's database, two dated 77, eleven dated 79, and three dated 80. Some MV vz. 70s were sold as surplus in the 1990s, but it is believed that the majority of them were involved in a large 2011 Czech arms sale to a South American buyer (David Pazdera, personal communication), probably a Brazilian surplus dealer, but the purchaser's identity has not been published.

36 The ČZ Models 50 and 70

Production History

Serial number 619444 was produced in 1980.

A triangle serial prefix was phased in beginning in 1979 to distinguish vz. 70s with serial numbers above 650000 from previously produced vz. 50s with identical numbers; serial number ∆664281 was produced in 1981.

Czech Cold War Police Pistols

Chapter 2

Serial number △719244 was produced in 1982.

Serial numbers in the 600000 range began to be used in late 1979, but by that point the order of assembly had become erratic; pistols with numbers from the 500000 serial block were still being accepted in 1980, as discussed below. Serial numbers from the 700000 serial block began to be used in 1981 and factory records indicate that the highest serial number applied was 724536 (David Pazdera, personal communication). Annual production figures for 1970 are not available but have been estimated from observations; other annual totals (Pazdera and Skramouššký 2006, 140–41) and observed serial ranges for the vz. 70 are provided in table 2-4.

As serial numbering approached the 650000 mark, ZUB management recognized that they would begin to duplicate those previously used on vz. 50s. It was decided to add a triangle prefix (possibly the Greek letter delta, which is used in mathematics to symbolize change), but implementation was spread over a broad serial number range, the earliest known example being 79-dated number △592259, and its use did not become general until 1980 at about number △644300. Even after this point the prefix was occasionally skipped and in 1982 its use apparently became sporadic, perhaps because factory workers knew that production was nearing its end, making the distinction less important. (On the basis of data available at the time, in 2009 the author attributed the triangle prefix to an internal change that affected parts compatibility, but additional data show that to have been an error; that internal change occurred in 1976.)

Probably in an effort to "clear the decks" for retooling in anticipation of shifting production to the new pistol that would become the military vz. 82 and commercial ČZ 83, in late 1979 the fabrication of vz. 70 receivers and parts was accelerated, building up a backlog of at least 65,000 serialized receiver-slide sets that evidently went into storage, to be withdrawn and assembled in more-or-less random order. This is not immediately evident in the 1980–81 serial number data, but in 1982 the randomization becomes quite obvious. Sixteen 82-dated pistols are currently recorded in the database, with serial numbers 660400, △697808, 708611, △711544, 718199, △718477, △719244, △719477, △719750, △721166, △721778, △722229, △722279, 722472, 722607, and △723234 embedded among the 81-dated serial numbers. The clustering of some of these numbers in the 718000–719000 and 721000–722000 serial blocks suggests that they came from the same pallet loads or cartloads of numbered receiver/slide sets, as would be expected. Two serial numbers above the listed factory endpoint have been reported, 81-dated

38   The ČZ Models 50 and 70

Production History

NB 52 serial number 737145 was rebuilt, refinished, and re-marked for commercial sale. Note "washed-out" slide markings and added MOD 50 designation.

△737909 and △738417; these may have been mistakes in transposition by the collectors who reported them, but they could also be factory numbering errors. All parts manufacturing apparently ended in 1981 and by 1982, all but one assembly line had been closed, completing about thirty pistols per day; production ended in early 1983. No 83-dated vz. 70s have been observed, but when found they will likely also be clustered and could come from anywhere in the 650000–724000 serial range (the acceptance date of serial number 724536, the reported factory endpoint, is currently unknown).

Pazdera and Skramoušský (2006, 140) place the total vz. 70 production at over 819,000, but this was a mathematical error that unfortunately was not recognized until after the book had gone to press (David Pazdera, personal communication). On the basis both of factory records and observed serial numbers, the actual total was approximately 745,000; adding 21,200 pistols from the D series to 724,536 (the total of the J series plus all six-digit serial numbers above 100000) yields a total of 745,736, which undoubtedly includes some pistols that failed to pass inspection and were rejected, validating the 745,000 estimate. When combined with the vz. 50 production estimate above, this yields an approximate grand total for both models of 1,102,623.

Beginning in 1979 and continuing through at least early 1982, older government-owned vz. 50s with significant service wear were recalled and re-furbished for commercial sale; vz 70s that had failed inspection due to mechanical issues were apparently included, either for adjustments to render them serviceable or as a source of spare parts. Many of the vz. 50s were upgraded to vz. 70 standards with new triggers, hammers, grip panels, magazines, and internal parts where needed; if barrels were replaced, the pistols were reproofed and dated on the left rear of the slide. External markings on these pistols often appear "washed out" from buffing prior to refinishing and slide legends may be illegible. Examples are NB 52–marked serial numbers 723053 and 737145; the latter evidently had its barrel replaced and was re-proofed with an 80 date. Due to their altered appearance, many of these pistols were stamped MOD 50 to clarify their identity for export purposes; some vz. 50s were erroneously stamped MOD 70 and in the US, BATFE denied pistols with this marking "Curio and Relic" status regardless of their production history, although this is being reconsidered as vz. 70s reach the age of fifty. The rebuilding work was not done at ZUB but was assigned to workshops and repair factories like those that rebuilt and refurbished Czech military arms.

Czech Cold War Police Pistols

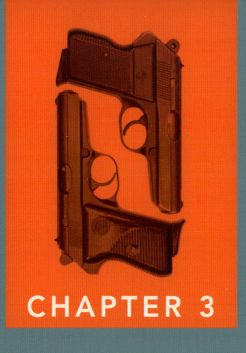

CHAPTER 3

Changes and Production Variations

During its lengthy production period, numerous manufacturing changes were made to the vz. 50-70 to improve handling characteristics, alleviate maintenance problems, and enhance production efficiency. Some changes were probably implemented during year-end breaks, when the factory was idled for the holidays and tooling could be adjusted or replaced without compromising operations, but both the "overlapping" phenomenon and the absence of specimens closely bracketing some changes make it difficult to be certain when they occurred. Internal changes are usually not visible in the photos used when offering these pistols for sale and since those photos are the primary source of the author's data, documenting internal changes has been challenging.

The first change occurred between 1950 serial number 677712 and 1951 serial number 688094. An oval 12 × 34 mm weight reduction cut in the front of the receiver below the barrel, 2 mm deep at its front, 6 mm deep at its rear, and part of the original design, was eliminated. This reduced manufacturing cost and because added weight in this area reduces the pistol's muzzle flip during recoil, it also offered a minor improvement in the shooter's control when firing, although the weight change was less than 0.5 ounce. Other than minor revisions of the slide-gripping grooves which are detailed below, this was the only design change noted during vz. 50 production at Strakonicé.

After the restart of manufacturing at ZUB a series of modifications appeared, partly in response to feedback from police officers using the pistols and interested in improving their handling qualities, and partly due to factory policy changes and efficiency measures. The first of these, implemented in 1958 between serial numbers B17407 and B19637, was the addition of fourteen fine vertical grooves to the front face of the trigger, which was originally smooth.

The weight-reduction cut seen below the barrel in serial number 652791 was eliminated before serial number 688094 was produced.

Changes and Production Variations

Smooth and grooved triggers

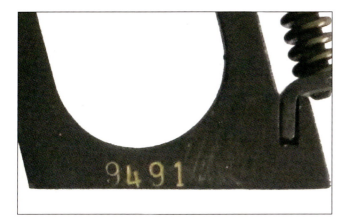

Control number on 1962 serial number B42327

In 1961 or 1962 a control number was added to the pistols' receivers, apparently as a theft prevention measure since no other parts carry it and, if an assembly number was needed, the last three or four serial number digits would have been adequate. The receivers of serial numbers B12078, B24998, and B31710 are not numbered, but B42327 carries the number 9491 on the outer face of the lower grip frame bridge, B42950 is numbered 11232, B55304 is numbered 5876, B62964 is numbered 3897, B67785 is numbered 5185, B69414 is numbered 20820, and other pistols dated 62 through 65 examined by the author also bear these markings, sometimes rendered illegible by buffing prior to finishing. Similar numbers appear on 6.35 mm Z pistols produced by ZUB in the early 1960s, so it was evidently a factory policy at that time. By 1967 serial number B85506, the practice had been discontinued and control numbers have not been observed on later pistols.

New, unfinished sideplate; note the absence of the sear pin and trigger pin holes and slide travel grooves. The sideplate would be bolted to an unfinished receiver, using the hammer pivot hole for drilling of the final pin holes and machining of the slide grooves and exterior contours for a precise fit.

Sideplates on vz. 50s were originally numbered to match the receiver, using the last three or four serial digits stamped in the inner trigger bar clearance recess or, less commonly, on the upper rear flat adjacent to the hammer. Final machining of the receiver was done with the sideplate attached so their external contours would match. When production was restarted at ZUB in 1957 these numbers were moved to the outside face of the sideplate, under the right grip panel. Sideplate serialization continued in the vz. 70 until at least 1976; 76-dated serial number 277218 carries it, while 77-dated 353659 and most later observed specimens do not. One 78-dated specimen described in chapter 5 has a sideplate serial but its full original number has been removed and replaced, preventing positive identification.

Safety levers on the vz. 50 may be found with varying lengths of the grooved gripping area, usually either 5.5 or 7.5 mm; this was apparently the result of slightly different settings on the tooling used to machine the flat on the safety body to the rear of the gripping area, rather than a planned change. "Long grip" safeties are more common on early vz. 50s, but "short grip" safeties have been observed as early as the 660000 serial range and are more common on vz. 50s produced at ZUB. Safeties on vz. 70s almost always have short grips.

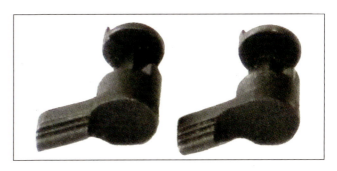

"Long grip" (*left*) and "short grip" safeties

Czech Cold War Police Pistols

Chapter 3

Inner faces of grip panels produced for Strakonicé (*top*) and ZUB vz. 50s

Original vz. 50 grip panels are made of black Bakelite plastic and are not serialized; those produced for the Strakonicé factory carry the encircled subcontractor's numbers 3727 (right side) or 3728 (left side) on their inside faces, along with the subcontractor's circular trademark, the horizontal word "ISOLIT" bisected by a vertical lightning bolt. Original ZUB grip panels are also made of black Bakelite but carry no subcontractor markings; ZUB factory replacement panels are made of dark-brown Bakelite and are also unmarked. Original grip panels for the vz. 70 are made of black styrene plastic without internal markings. (After-market replacement panels are produced by several manufacturers and are usually made of urethane or other polymers; they may appear in any color and may carry the manufacturer's identification or copies of markings that were on the original panels from which their molds were made.) The right panels are vulnerable to breakage at the upper rear corner due to the reduced thickness over the hammer pivot nut; this problem is exacerbated by exposure to wear in open-top police holsters. All Bakelite panels are brittle and easily chipped or broken when impacted or dropped. Original right panels have a brass escutcheon for the grip screw molded in place; reproduction panels usually lack this feature and require a separate escutcheon or nut for attachment.

Grip screws for the vz. 50 are 27 mm long; in the vz. 70 they were shortened to 26 mm to match the flatter cross-section of the revised grip panels. The vz. 50 screws will fit both models, although they protrude slightly from the right side of vz. 70 grips and can cause minor discomfort to shooters; vz. 70 screws may not fit vz. 50 grip panels, depending on individual panel thickness. Vz. 70 screws also will not fit some custom wooden panels.

Examples of serial numerals used at Strakonicé, 1950–52

Examples of serial numerals used at ZUB, 1957–67

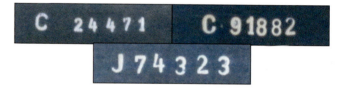

Examples of serial numerals used at ZOB, 1968–73

The dies used for serial numbering varied both in size and style over time. Those used at Strakonicé had broad-based 1s and flat-topped 3s but they may be either 2 mm or 2.5 mm in height, even on the same pistol. Dies used at ZUB had round-topped 3s; those used through mid-1967 were 2 mm high and had 1s without base serifs, but those in use in late 1967 had 1s with narrow base serifs. In early 1968 the C prefix was enlarged to 3 mm, but the numerals remained the same; later that year, between serial numbers C60289 and C63160, the numerals were enlarged to 3 mm, although their style remained unchanged through 1973. By mid-1974 the numeral style had again changed, using 1s without base serifs and 7s that had vertically flattened upper right corners. By mid-1978, 1s again had base serifs and 7s had pointed corners. Both factories used open-topped 4s, but this was more pronounced in numerals used at ZUB than those from Strakonicé. Numerals used for proof dating often differ from those used for serialization; most, if not all, ZUB proof dates were stamped with two-digit dies, which is apparent when the date is not evenly stamped; if the bottom (or top) of one digit is shallow, the corresponding part of the other digit will also be shallow.

Examples of serial numerals used at ZUB, 1974–77

Examples of serial numerals used at ZUB, 1978–83

Left to right, smooth machined, rough machined, smooth "forged," and impressed pattern slide rib variants

The sighting rib on early vz. 50 slides may be either smooth- or rough-machined, leaving semicircular tool marks; this is simply an artifact of the tooling used and how recently the milling cutter had been sharpened and adjusted. Pistols produced at ZUB through 1962 have similar sighting ribs, but following the 1964 relocation tool marks are usually not visible except at the rear of the front sight base. It appears that the factory began using slide forgings at that time rather than machining them from bar stock, since the slide rib surface has the slightly gritty texture typical of steel forgings. This would be a logical change, since the forging could include part of the barrel channel in the bottom of the slide, significantly reducing machining requirements; a period when production machinery was being relocated would also be ideal for reorienting the tooling to handle preshaped forgings, but the author has been unable to verify that this was done. (Note that this is an unproven theory; 64-dated serial number 45178 and 65-dated B66899 and B69414 have slide ribs with semicircular tool marks but they may be examples of overlapping, using slides fabricated before the 1963 operational suspension. Only factory records can verify or disprove the theory.) Beginning in mid-1967, sighting ribs were impressed with a lengthwise nonreflecting wave pattern except for a 9 mm flat immediately behind the front sight; this pattern remained in use through the end of production. The lowest observed serial number with the wave pattern rib is C01562, while the highest number with the smooth "forged" rib is C02239.

The vz. 50 prototype hammer had a sharp spur with three lateral gripping grooves; in production pistols this was changed to a more rounded shape with seven gripping grooves, probably to avoid snagging on undercover officers' clothing when drawn from a shoulder holster. However, a significant number of prototype hammers had been fabricated before the "official" start of production and rather than wasting them, they were put to use and are scattered randomly throughout Strakonicé production. Examples are NB 50–marked serial numbers 651682, 653071, 658054, 668122, 693971, 695952; NB 51–marked 704100; and NB 52–marked 737590. Occurrence in the database suggests that they were used on about 750 Strakonicé vz. 50s. In 1967, near the end of the B series, the rounded solid hammer was replaced by a ring type with a chamfered 4 mm diameter hole and eight deep gripping grooves; the lowest observed

Chapter 3

NB 50 serial number 658054 is equipped with the prototype hammer

serial number with the ring hammer is B98503, but there is a data gap of about 8,000 serial numbers below that, leaving the change point in doubt. There was evidently significant overlapping and the highest observed number with the solid hammer is C18630. In early 1970, the "large" 4 mm hole hammer was replaced by a "small" 3 mm hole version with seven gripping grooves; the highest observed serial number with the large-hole hammer is D07617, while the lowest with the small hole is D01822. The probable reasons for adopting the first ring hammer were improved thumb grip during cocking and a more modern appearance, but the reasons for the change to the second ring type are unclear; both types of ring hammers weigh 21 g, while the early solid type weighs 22 g. On both types of ring hammers, the amount of chamfering of the ring hole varies randomly from almost non-existent to a diameter of up to 7 mm. The only logical explanation is that the chamfering was intended only to remove sharp edges from the hole but was done with manually controlled machinery, so the chamfering depth depended on the operator's mood, haste, or attention to detail at the time.

Hammer variants, *from left*: prototype, early solid, large-hole ring, small-hole ring

44   The ČZ Models 50 and 70

Changes and Production Variations

1970-dated serial number C95444 is the lowest observed with the checkered disassembly button.

The original disassembly button has an arched face with seven vertical grooves. At the beginning of 1970 the button was redesigned, giving it a flat face with stamped checkering. The highest observed serial number with the grooved face is 69-dated D03897, while the lowest with the checkered button is 70-dated C95444. A transitional flat, horizontally grooved button may exist but has not been confirmed; it is discussed in chapter 5.

In August 1967 between serial numbers C02861 and C05333, a leaf spring acting through a 6 × 10 mm oval slot in the rear grip frame was added to apply friction to the rear of the magazine, preventing it from falling free when released. The slot for this spring was enlarged to 7 × 10 mm in the D series and to an 8 × 10 mm opening incorporated in the frame forging in 1973. Addition of the magazine-retaining spring required a clearance channel to be incorporated into the front face of the hammer spring retainer; early-type hammer spring retainers will not accept magazine retaining springs. (Serial number C18630 was evidently assembled when this change was in the process of being implemented and new parts had not been distributed, possibly before number C05333 due to "overlapping," since its receiver is cut for the magazine-retaining spring but it was assembled with the unmodified hammer spring retainer and no magazine retaining spring.) A number of earlier National Security Corps vz. 50s were retrofitted with magazine-retaining springs; examples are serial numbers 698137, 707141, and 737145, but this can be determined only through direct examination of pistols, making estimates of the number of conversions from the database impossible.

Changes were made repeatedly to the slide-gripping grooves in an effort to enhance the shooter's grip during manual operation. Initially, fifteen diagonal grooves were machined into both sides of the slide, beginning 16 mm forward of the bottom rear corner and providing a gripping length of 22 mm. On early pistols the grooves were 0.5 mm wide, slightly narrower than the lands between them, with a square cross section. (On some very early pistols the lands

Czech Cold War Police Pistols

Chapter 3

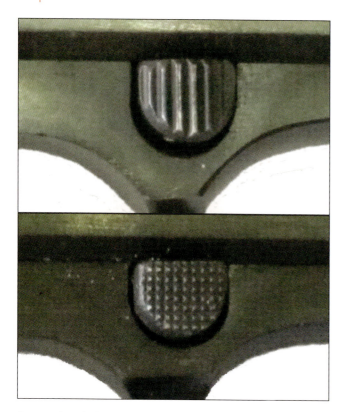

Grooved and checkered disassembly buttons

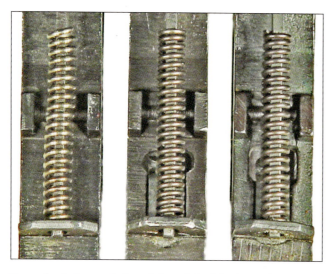

Rear of grip frame, *left to right*: original design without magazine retaining spring, modified design with retaining spring in machined recess, late frame with retaining spring in larger recess incorporated in the frame forging

Left to right: early hammer spring retainer without channel, modified hammer spring retainer with channel, magazine retaining spring. The rounded end of the spring to the right presses against the magazine.

vary in size, narrow at the rear and increasing in width toward the front, but this appears to have been the result of a "learning curve" as factory technicians adjusted the machinery for uniform width; see photo of serial number 650564 in chapter 2.) By the 660000 serial range (lowest observed example is serial number 658054), the grooves had been enlarged to 0.7 mm, retaining the square cross section, making them wider than the lands between them; this change is very difficult to see without using a magnifying measuring device such as a thread comparator. During the 730000 serial range the cross section was changed from square to V shaped, with the diagonal surface at the front; this widened the grooves to 0.9 mm, further narrowing the lands. When production was restarted at ZUB in 1957 the fifteen V-shaped grove pattern was retained and remained unchanged for about ten years. In 1967 between serial numbers C00440 and C01562, the length of the grooved surface was increased from 22 to 32 mm, starting 10 mm forward of the lower rear slide corner; the size and shape of the grooves were unchanged although their spacing increased slightly, producing a twenty-one-groove slide. This slide groove pattern was short lived; between serial numbers C02861 and C03584 the grooves were widened and their number was reduced to sixteen, retaining the 32 mm gripping length and moving the starting point to 8 or 9 mm forward of the lower rear slide corner (there are minor variations in this distance, probably due to random variances in tool settings). It is possible that the original plan was to extend the gripping length from 22 to 32 mm and enlarge the grooves at the same time, but since the larger grooves required new tooling the gripping length was temporarily extended using the original size of grooves for trial purposes while the new cutter was being made. The width of the enlarged grooves is 1.2 mm and the lands between them 0.8 mm, retaining the V shape. With the vz. 70 model change, the starting point of the grooves was moved forward to 19 mm from the lower rear slide corner to allow room for the ČZ logo on the left rear of the slide, and it remained in that position through the end of production.

Slide serial numbers were originally stamped below the extractor groove, centered between the gripping grooves and the ejection port. The introduction of the twenty-one-groove slide moved the serial number forward about 9 mm and the vz. 70 model change again pushed it forward. By 1974, the number had migrated to the point where it was

Changes and Production Variations

First slide grip variation, fifteen grooves with lands wider than the grooves, 22 mm gripping length

Second slide grip variation with fifteen grooves slightly wider than the lands, 22 mm gripping length

Third slide grip variation with fifteen V-shaped rather than square grooves, 22 mm gripping length

Fourth slide grip variation with twenty-one V-shaped grooves, 32 mm gripping length

Fifth slide grip variation with sixteen V-shaped grooves, 32 mm gripping length

Sixth slide grip variation with the same sixteen grooves moved forward 10 mm

directly below the ejection port and it retained that position for the balance of production, although there was variability both in the location and spacing of numerals; no effort appears to have been made to align the slide and receiver numbering.

The most-visible changes introduced in the vz. 70 were to the grip panels and magazine floorplate finger rest. The original grip panels had twenty-two horizontal grooves starting one-third of the way down the side and continuing to the bottom, their length increasing from top to bottom to form a semicircular pattern; the ČZ logo was molded into the upper part of the right panel. In the vz. 70, the panels were given a trapezoidal enclosure covering the lower three-quarters of their sides with a raised diamond gripping surface; grooves extended around the rear edges and the ČZ logo was retained on the upper part of the right panel. The rear contour was modified to improve the pistol's pointing quality, raising the muzzle about 5 degrees when gripped normally. The original vz. 50 magazine floor plate was provided with a black or dark-brown Bakelite extension with a downward-curved front tip forming a finger rest: in the vz. 70 the finger rest was made thicker and more angular to resist breakage. Magazines were also produced without finger rests to make them more compact; this type is less common but it is the only one that fits the separate single magazine pouches issued with shoulder holsters and compact belt holsters.

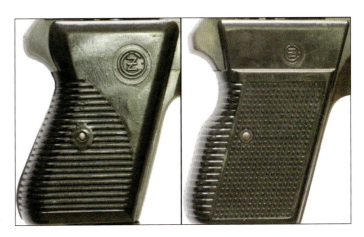

Vz. 50 (*left*) and vz. 70 grip panels, right side

Czech Cold War Police Pistols

There are five variants of the standard magazine with finger rest, labeled for purposes of discussion as types 1 through 5; the corresponding compact magazines without finger rests would thus be labeled 1a through 5a, as discussed below. All magazines are completely interchangeable, but because they were often separated from pistols during the importation process (sometimes sold separately to generate extra revenue) and later randomly replaced, collectors may wish to properly match magazines to specific pistols. (Estimated "change" dates are based on pistols that are known to have been imported singly and can thus be assumed to retain their original magazines.) Magazine bodies are formed from .032" steel with the rear folded double and spot-welded at four points, usually but not always visible; the original design had a cut for the magazine catch in the upper right front and seven 5 mm diameter cartridge-counter holes on the left side. Magazine followers are shaped like an inverted U, with 15 mm extensions at the front and rear that contact the inside of the body to ensure proper alignment; they are normally polished "white," although blued followers are occasionally encountered due to refinishing. **Type 1** magazines, with the original body, plain follower, and the vz. 50 finger rest described above, were supplied with all vz. 50s produced at Strakonicé and those from ZUB through 1963. Probably at the restart of production in 1964 (the exact point is difficult to establish due to overlapping and magazine separation during importation), a beveled horizontal notch that is 5 mm wide and 1 mm deep was stamped into the forward left inside of the follower top, probably as a clamping or indexing point for the tooling used to shape it; this change created the **type 2** magazine. Probably in early 1967 (the exact timing is again difficult to establish for the reasons noted), an eighth 4 mm hole was added to the body below the cartridge counters and closer to the magazine's centerline, allowing a tool to be inserted to restrain

Magazine follower variants, *left to right*: original; 1964 modification with undercut notch; 1976 modification with beveled left front corner

Magazine body variants: original seven-hole (*left*) and 1967 modified eight-hole

Magazine finger rests: vz. 50 (*left*) and vz. 70

the follower while the inside of the magazine is being cleaned, creating the **type 3**. The revised finger rest introduced with the vz. 70 model change created the **type 4**; there was no change to the compact magazines at that time, so no distinct type 4a exists. When the hold-open catch was modified in 1976, the magazine follower was redesigned to accommodate its larger magazine contact lug by eliminating the indexing notch and stamping a 2 mm wide beveled face into the top left front corner, creating the **type 5**. This modification was actually unnecessary since pistols with the modified catch will feed reliably from type 4 magazines but manufacturing of the type 5 continued until the end of vz. 70 production. There were apparently very few type 5a magazines produced, probably because by 1976 the demand

Changes and Production Variations

Standard magazines, *left to right*, types 1 through 5

Compact magazines without finger rest, *left to right*, types 1a, 2a, 3a, and 5a; there is no distinct type 4a.

for compact magazines had declined to the point where existing stocks were adequate; the author has encountered only one example in his collecting career. An estimated 3–5 percent of the standard magazines examined by the author do not conform to the type descriptions and have follower, body, and base combinations that are irregular; some of these are the result of repair or rebuilding, but others appear to be in unissued condition without evidence of modification. This is apparently due to the overlapping phenomenon, since the stamped magazine bodies and followers were much easier

Chapter 3

to fabricate than milled parts and were thus produced intermittently in large batches that were replenished when needed, allowing stocks of "old" components to remain in inventory and mix with "new" components longer than usual. Collectors should use logic in deciding whether these irregular magazines are correct for a particular pistol; a magazine with a vz. 50 finger rest, an eight-hole body, and an early follower should be considered an irregular type 3 or, if you wish, type 3i; a magazine with a vz. 70 finger rest, either type of body, and an early or intermediate notched follower should be considered an irregular type 4 or type 4i. Most magazines are unmarked, although some type 5 magazines carry a 2 mm triangle similar to the serial prefix introduced in 1979 stamped near the bottom of the rear face; no direct relationship between this magazine marking and the serial prefix is known. Type 5 magazines may also carry an encircled TK over 62 in the same position; this stands for *technicá kontrola* ("skilled inspection"), with the number identifying the inspecting authority. Magazines are not serialized unless added by the purchaser, but some type 5s carry the numeral 1 stamped on the bottom rear, possibly to identify the "first" and "second" magazines at the purchaser's request. No magazines with the numeral 2 have been observed, but the Czechs could have utilized a "1 and none" marking scheme similar to the "dot and no dot" magazine markings used on Nambu military pistols by imperial Japan. However, since these markings appear only on type 5 magazines made late in the production period, this is unlikely.

Another modification introduced with the vz. 70 was a change in the receiver contour at its junctions with the trigger guard. In the vz. 50 these junctions are angular, but in the vz. 70 they are concavely rounded, marginally improving trigger finger access and giving the pistol more of a sleek, streamlined

Vz. 50 receiver contours at trigger guard

Examples of vz. 70 magazine markings

Vz. 70 receiver contours at trigger guard

50   The ČZ Models 50 and 70

appearance. As a result, the area at the left front of the trigger guard where the proof is stamped, which is flat in the vz. 50, is concave in the vz. 70, making the impression less distinct. In addition, the vz. 70's trigger guard is 1.5 mm deeper than the vz. 50's, which can affect the pistol's fit in holsters and some other containers. Metal removed by the revised contours, together with the enlarged magazine-retaining spring recess, contributes to the vz. 70's slightly lower weight.

The original hammer pivot had a small indentation in one side of its head that engaged a key in the receiver recess to prevent the pivot from turning when its nut was being installed or removed; the threaded end of the pivot had a small slot cut in its lower front, just to the left of the threads, to accommodate the trigger bar. In 1971, between serial numbers J14191 and J16538, the hammer pivot head was modified to a conventional slotted screw style and the receiver key was eliminated, although the edge of the recess was usually staked to prevent the pivot from turning; the shoulder abutting the threaded section near the right end of the pivot was set back about 2 mm to replace the clearance slot for the trigger bar. There was probably significant overlapping of this change, but since the pivot head is hidden under the left grip panel, observations from photos are difficult to obtain.

Early (*left*) and late hammer pivot heads

Threaded ends of early (*left*) and late hammer pivots with the right shoulder slotted or set back to accommodate the trigger bar

The hold-open catch for the slide, which has a raised step that serves as the ejector, is a bar that is 66 mm long, pivoting around a transverse pin under the front of the chamber and operated by a coil spring housed in a vertical receiver recess and by interaction with the magazine follower. Originally, contact with the magazine follower was through a spur projecting to the right into the magazine well through a receiver cut that is 4 mm wide and 2.5 mm deep. The upper face of this spur was tapered to a point to prevent it from interfering with cartridges being fed from the magazine into the chamber, but this made it fragile and easily broken. In 1976, between serial numbers 278203 and 321937, the spur was changed to a flange 4.5 mm long from front to rear, extending 3.5 mm into the magazine well; the rear of the catch was also modified to strengthen it and reduce impact damage to the cartridge head recess in the breech face. The receiver cut into the magazine well was enlarged to 7 mm long by 4 mm deep to accommodate the revised catch and was incorporated into the receiver forging; the magazine follower was also given a 2 mm wide relief cut in its left front corner, as noted above, to prevent the hold-open catch lug from interfering with the last cartridge being fed from the magazine.

Receiver and sideplate contours at the rear grip tang varied considerably during production. The vertical face at the rear of the tang, measured from the bottom of the hammer recess to the lower tang corner, is approximately 8 mm in early pistols and as little as 3.5 mm in later ones. The differences were evidently the result of a series of minor tooling adjustments, but they affect both the pistol's weight and handling and produce significant contrasts when receivers and sideplates from different production periods are mated (see photo of "hybrid" vz. 50-70 at end of chapter 7).

Early (*lower*) and late hold-open catches

Chapter 3

Early (*front*) and late hold-open catch magazine contacts

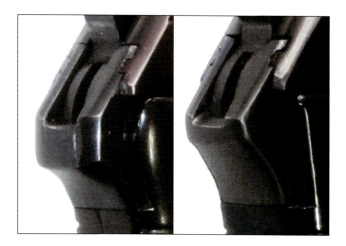

Examples of large and small rear grip tang faces

Examples of vz. 50 encircled caliber variations, *left to right, top row*: 1950, 1958, 1962; *bottom row*: 1964, 1968, 1970

There are minor variations in the encircled caliber markings on the slides of vz. 50s, both in numeral style and in the size of numerals to the left and right of the comma. On pistols produced at Strakonicé the markings are consistent, but several different styles were used at ZUB. These differences are minor and were obviously not planned changes—probably merely whimsical modifications by tool- and die-makers—but they may be of interest to collectors who appreciate nuances. There are also minor differences in the encircled ČZ trademark.

The finish on early vz. 50s was hot-salts bluing, with the exception of the trigger pin, magazine follower, and the exposed left face of the cartridge indicator, which were left "white" or, in the case of the cartridge indicator, sometimes heat-treated to a straw or plum color. Treatment of trigger pins and cartridge indicators became variable in early 1970, either white or blued without a discernible pattern. Safety indicator recesses in the left side of the receiver were colored with a spot of red paint. Strakonicé vz. 50s from the 670000–692000 serial

52   The ČZ Models 50 and 70

range are often found with plum-colored slides; this is the result of high manganese content in the steel that was used and was not intentional. The manganese coloring takes time to "bloom" after the slide is blued—often several years—and probably was not noticeable when the pistols were produced. The plum finish is less durable than ordinary blued steel and will often fade to pale pink or tan from holster or pocket wear while the rest of the pistol's finish remains intact. ZUB vz. 50s are occasionally seen with nickel plating, usually police trade-ins; these pistols were probably plated by the purchaser, not the factory (the author has been unable to confirm any factory plating of vz. 50s). ZUB produced some special-order vz. 70s with nickel or gold plating or highlighting, but they are uncommon. Both models are occasionally found with a phosphate finish (Parkerizing); an example is 64-dated serial number B55348, imported by Cole Distributing Inc. of Scottsville, Kentucky. Czech sources state that Parkerizing was not used on pistols by ZUB during the vz. 50-70 production period, so the author contacted the importer, inquired about the pistol's finish, and learned that they had bead-blasted and Parkerized several small lots of vz. 50s with extensive finish wear and light surface pitting to enhance marketability. Vz. 50-70s are also occasionally encountered with "two-tone" finishes, usually with the slide blued and the receiver polished "white" or nickeled; this is not factory work but was done by the importer or a previous owner.

In late 1982 and early 1983, an effort may have been made to "dress up" vz. 70s as the end of production approached. Serial number708611, dated 82, has the chamber and the outer faces of the hammer and trigger polished "white." The chamber polishing was done with the sideplate removed and the hammer and trigger polishing obviously had to be done with the pistol disassembled. When acquired this pistol was in almost unfired condition, but it was coated with hardened oil that cemented the parts together and prevented them from moving, evidently from protracted storage in a warm, dry environment. The seller thought the dried oil was rust, had broken the magazine finger rest in an effort to remove the magazine, and sold the pistol at a modest price as a "parts gun," but after purchasing it and soaking it in solvent for several hours the author was able to loosen the slide enough with a rubber mallet to remove it; the pistol could then be disassembled, cleaned, and restored. It had been imported from Germany and carried a Waffen Frankonia Würtzberg import stamp, but it is impossible to determine whether the polishing was done by the factory or by a purchaser who then coated it with oil and left it unattended for an extended period of time. (It seems illogical that a purchaser would do this, but circumstantial evidence alone proves nothing.) Illustrations on both versions of the vz. 70 commercial box appear to show pistols with similar polished parts, suggesting that this treatment was at least contemplated at some point. Pazdera and Skramoušský (2006, 141) provide a photo of the left side of a vz. 70 with a gold-plated hammer and trigger, evidently from the ČZ factory collection, but its serial number and acceptance date are not visible and no explanation is provided for the unusual treatment. The absence of a serial prefix suggests that number 708611 was accepted "late" in 1982, but without access to factory archives, validation of its treatment as original can be validated only by examining 83-dated pistols when they appear.

Chapter 3

NB 50 serial number 672712 with plum slide coloration

1964-dated serial number B55348 was Parkerized by the importer

Changes and Production Variations

1982-dated serial number 708611 with polished chamber, hammer, and trigger

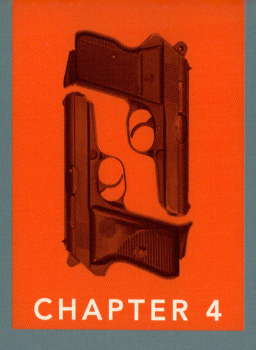

CHAPTER 4

Marking Variations and Foreign Markings

Prototype serial number 006 slide markings, from the first vz. 50 instruction manual

First marking variation

Early vz. 50 prototypes vary significantly from production pistols, but "final" prototype 006 is identical to Strakonicé production pistols in most respects. It has walnut grip panels, a round magazine catch button, and the spur hammer described in chapter 3, while the slide carries a two-line inscription bracketed by the ČZ logo on the left and encircled 7,65 caliber designation on the right. Although the prototype is permanently retained in the Czech Republic, artists' renditions of this pistol used on early boxes, instruction manuals, and promotional materials were prepared before production of the vz. 50 actually began, so the prototype was used as a model and its slide legend appears on these items.

Six marking variations were used on production pistols, the first three evolving at Strakonicé with marketing and management changes. The **first marking variation** is a two-line abbreviation of the prototype marking, used on the left side of the slides of pistols produced in 1950 through about serial number 680500, with some overlapping. As noted earlier, commercial pistols carry the proof and acceptance date on the left side of the slide forward of the gripping grooves, while government pistols carry the acceptance date and agency identification on the front grip strap. A second proof is stamped on the right side of the receiver over the chamber and the serial number is stamped on the right side of the chamber below the proof, visible through the ejection port, and on the right side of the slide below the extractor.

Second marking variation

Marking Variations and Foreign Markings

Third marking variation

In late 1950, beginning at about serial number 680500 with significant overlapping, the national-origin line MADE IN CZECHOSLOVAKIA was added to the left side of the receiver below the slide legend using 1 mm letters, creating the **second marking variation**. The absence of the national-origin line with the original slide legend probably reflects the emphasis of early production on the government contracts, since it had been used on 6.35 mm vz. 45 pistols produced at Strakonicé since 1947.

Beginning in 1951 at about serial number 711500 (with significant overlapping) and continuing through the end of production in 1952, the slide legend was changed to a single line reflecting supervisory authority rather than the factory location, while retaining the national-origin line on the receiver; this is the **third marking variation**. Commercial pistols with the first three marking variations are considerably less common in the US than government contract pistols; this is partly due to the larger number of government pistols produced, but it also reflects the fact that the majority of Czech government vz. 50s were later sold as surplus on US markets, while commercial pistols were widely dispersed through international sales and some of them probably remain in service.

With the restart of production at ZUB in 1957 the slide legend reverted to two lines, replacing the company name and location with the model number and moving the national-origin line from the receiver to the slide, creating the **fourth marking variation**. The production date and proof were moved to the left side of the slide, to the rear of the cartridge indicator, with a second proof stamped on the left side of the receiver at the top front of the trigger guard.

Fourth marking variation

Fifth marking variation

The vz. 69 prototype carried a unique slide legend that included the caliber designation, with the ČZ logo enlarged to 8.5 mm and moved to the rear of the gripping grooves. It is not considered a legitimate variation because these pistols were never produced commercially, but without alterations other than changing the model number from 69 to 70, it became the **fifth marking variation**.

Fifth- (*left*) and sixth-variation serial numbers

Beginning in 1979, the addition of the triangle serial prefix created the **sixth marking variation**. Although most vz. 70s produced in 1980–82 carry this prefix, it was occasionally skipped and in 1982 its use became sporadic; thus, both fifth- and sixth-variation pistols may be encountered with dates from 1979 through 1982. Whether the prefix continued to be used or was dropped completely in 1983 is currently unknown. Estimates of production numbers for all six marking variations are provided in table 4-1.

Table 4-1	Estimated Production by Marking Variation
Variation 1	34,513
Variation 2	27,500
Variation 3	26,810
Variation 4	268,800
Variation 5	578,000
Variation 6	167,000
Total	1,102,623

Czech Cold War Police Pistols

It is interesting to note that while the type markings on these pistols are in the Czech language, the national-origin lines both on the pistols and their boxes are always in English. This is ironic, considering that during the entire production period of the vz. 50-70, Czechoslovakia was politically aligned against the world's English-speaking nations.

Foreign Markings

Due to their quality and widespread commercial distribution, Czech arms have been imported by many nations both for police and military use and, where allowed, for private purchase. Although Czech firearms were proofed before leaving the factory, the laws of some countries require reproofing of foreign-made firearms when they are imported and some military and police organizations mark their weapons so they can be identified if lost or stolen. The resulting proofs and property marks can serve as "tracks" to help purchasers of surplus arms trace at least some parts of their history.

Ulm, West Germany, proofs on 1962 vz. 50 serial number B42327. The BRIGANT trade name is stamped on the grip frame below the magazine catch.

German import mark of Waffen Frankonia Würzberg is stamped on the receiver just forward of the magazine catch on 1971 vz. 70 serial number J08375.

West Germany was one of the countries that required proofing of imported firearms and even during the Cold War era, when trade between Warsaw Pact and NATO member countries was restricted, the German firm Waffen Frankonia Würzberg was able to arrange purchases of many Czech pistols. These pistols often—but not always—carry German commercial proofs; they also carry the firm's import mark (⚜) in sizes ranging from 1 to 8 mm in height, and they usually also carry the trade name *BRIGANT*. US military and diplomatic personnel serving in Germany often purchased these pistols and brought them home; some of them have also been commercially imported.

Cuba purchased vz. 50s for its army in 1970, although the quantity is unknown, and most of them probably remain in service along with the island nation's antique automobiles and other outdated equipment. Serial number D36724 carries Cuban army markings on the right side of its slide and was probably brought into the US by clandestine means; no other pistols with these markings are known.

Discrete US import marking under the right grip panel of vz. 50 serial number B85506

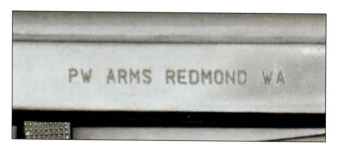

Most US import markings are intended to be plainly visible

Dot-matrix replacement serial number applied by a US importer

Marking Variations and Foreign Markings

Cuban army–marked serial number D36724. *Robert E. Hogan collection and photo*

Duplicate import serial number applied to 1972 vz. 70 number 105160; the logic behind this requirement appears irrational.

Under the terms of the 1968 Gun Control Act firearms imported into the US must meet certain size limitations, intended to bar the entry of small, cheap "Saturday night specials," a term coined by antigun politicians, and they must be stamped with the importer's identification and location to facilitate ownership tracing if they are involved in a crime. Early import markings were often designed to be discrete, not marring the firearm's appearance, and some importers placed them under grip panels or in other locations where they would not impair collector interest. However, other importers use large, unsightly markings that detract from the firearm's appearance and make it less appealing to collectors. In some cases, pistols that have legitimate and legible type markings and serial numbers have these markings, or substitutes for them, restamped in large, dot-matrix characters, presumably at the direction of BATFE. Unfortunately, import markings are sometimes applied to a pistol's front grip strap, obscuring original government markings on vz. 50s produced at Strakonicé. Altering or removing these marks is, of course, prohibited.

Century Arms International (C.A.I.), which is both a firearms importer and manufacturer, was a major importer of surplus Czech pistols when they were released in the early 1990s. At that time the company was located in St. Albans, Vermont, as indicated by their import markings, but in 2000 they relocated their corporate office to Florida and their import markings were changed to Georgia, Vermont, the location of their manufacturing plant. In 2019, they moved the location of the import markings on pistols from the side of the slide to the bottom of the trigger guard, probably to reduce visual impact, but these changes allow owners to determine the approximate periods when their pistols were imported.

Czech Cold War Police Pistols

Chapter 4

During the 1970s the Irish Republican Army (IRA) terrorist organization purchased vz. 70 pistols directly from Czechoslovakia, removing their serial numbers to prevent them from being traced if confiscated by British authorities. One of these pistols, dated 78, had both its receiver and slide numbers removed with a milling machine, leaving neat, oval slots about 2 mm deep where they had been; it was later deactivated by drilling a hole into its chamber. It is in the collection of the (British) National Army Museum and photos can be viewed at https://collection.nam.ac.uk/detail.php?acc=1993-04-389-1. While it is unlikely that any former IRA weapons are in the US, both the United Kingdom and the European Union allow private individuals to possess pistols that have been "officially deactivated"; observed specimens are marked **EU** over **GB** or **EU** followed by **AT**, with other proof-like markings, so it is possible that they could turn up here.

One of the largest procurements of Czech vz. 50-70s was an arrangement known in the US as the "African Contract." These pistols carry a stamped or engraved mark on the right side of their slides, forward of the serial number, resembling the letters "dP" with their vertical strokes joined (ᛝ). Like most foreign purchases, the contract was handled through the Ministry of Foreign Trade (MZO) and details have not been released, but one of the earliest purchasers of vz. 50s was Abyssinia (modern Ethiopia) and they may have been the party involved, although the number of pistols included suggests that if so, they may have served as a distributor to several other African nations. South Africa is also known to have purchased vz. 50-70s and produced cotton-webbing holsters for them; two examples are pictured in chapter 8. However, a South Africa firearms source contacted by the author was unfamiliar with the mark and did not believe it was used there; the

"African Contract" property mark

60   The CZ Models 50 and 70

Marking Variations and Foreign Markings

"X" property mark, origin unknown

South African military property mark used until 1961 was an adaptation of the British "broad arrow" under a dome. Large numbers of African Contract vz. 70s appear in the database dated 72, 80, and 81; smaller numbers appear in the middle 70s, and a few Strakonicé vz. 50s are also contract-marked, although they are all also NB marked and were evidently included in purchases after being declared surplus. About 14 percent of all vz. 70s in the database are contract-marked, indicating that it probably represents the largest purchase of vz. 50-70s in history, although some extensive data gaps could also represent large foreign purchases of pistols that remain in service or for other reasons have not made their way to US markets. The African Contract pistols were evidently sold here en mass when they were declared surplus and are thus overrepresented in the database, making estimates of their total number unreliable. It would be interesting to know more about the service lives of these pistols, but efforts to learn such details have thus far proved futile.

The author purchased 81-dated vz. 70 serial number △699715 in 2007, imported by C.A.I. in the 1990s, because it carried an "X" stamped just forward of the slide number, apparently as a property mark. For more than a decade, no other pistols with this mark appeared on any of the firearms auction websites, but eleven more X-marked vz. 70s were offered in 2020, all imported by C.A.I. and dated 72 through 76, but with the property mark adjacent to the receiver serial rather than on the slide. The pistols appeared as scattered singles rather than in clusters, suggesting a number of small procurements. To date, the purchaser has not been identified.

Another group of pistols with unusual markings appeared in 2020, carrying a 3 mm tall, 2 mm wide bullet-shaped mark, round at the top and flat at the bottom, on the right side of both the receiver and slide, accompanied by a two-digit year date. These marks are usually too lightly stamped to show detail, but the interior contains an irregular diagonal line from upper left to lower right, probably representing a mountain slope,

Czech Cold War Police Pistols

Chapter 4

1982-dated vz. 70 serial number 660400 with 2002-dated Peruvian markings; only the stylized Chinchura tree is recognizable.

National crest of Peru

with a symmetrical tree bearing four branches on the upper right. To date, fifteen vz. 70s and twelve vz. 50s (some retrofitted with vz. 70 grip panels) carrying these marks have been recorded, one with dual markings and two different dates. Czech acceptance dates on these pistols cover almost the entire production period from 1950 to 1982 and one has a star serial prefix, while the added marking dates range from 00 to 13 (2000 to 2013), so the pistols had been sold as surplus before being re-marked. An internet search of national crests and coats of arms yielded the crest of Peru, with a conventionally shaped shield bordered by wreaths and adorned with a stylized Chinchura tree on the upper right, a vicuña (the wild progenitor of the domestic alpaca) on the upper left, and a cornucopia spilling gold coins at the bottom, the tree apparently being the object on the bullet-shaped mark. The shape, dating, and double marking with different dates on one pistol suggest that these are probably proofs, but that has not been verified; they could also be property marks from a Peruvian police agency.

Marking Variations and Foreign Markings

Property markings on vz. 50 serial number C00024

Some national and municipal police agencies mark weapons and other equipment, but these markings may be difficult to identify. 1967-dated serial number C00024 carries these marks on the chamber and the right side of the receiver surrounding the disassembly button, but they are too lightly stamped to be seen clearly. They appear to be an oval enclosing an image of a stag's head, a cross with letters in its four quadrants that are mostly illegible, and the inventory number 0181.

One recurring property mark consists of the letters TRA, stamped on the right side of the receiver. Six of these have been observed, widely scattered on pistols dated from 72 to 79, suggesting repeated small procurements, but the purchaser's identity is unknown. Since the language from which the letters are drawn is also not known, speculation about their meaning is pointless.

Some markings invite speculation. As an example, 74-dated vz. 70 receiver serial number 183624 is mated with slide number 183552 and both the receiver and slide are stamped ZA-312 on the left side. Regardless of how and where the receiver and slide mismatching occurred, the owner evidently wanted to signify that they were officially united as pistol #312 in their inventory. The former owner's identity, of course, is anyone's guess.

Czech Cold War Police Pistols

63

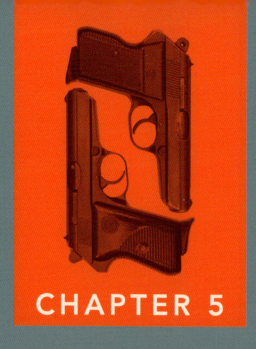

CHAPTER 5

Anomalies, Oddities, and Unique Specimens

With more than 1.1 million vz. 50-70s having been produced and many of them later rebuilt, refurbished, or modified by their owners, it is not surprising that specimens appear with unusual markings and features. The factories that produced them built some special-purpose and trial pistols and even during normal operations, factory and workshop errors occurred that were either missed during final inspection or ignored because they did not affect the pistol's serviceability. Some pistols were modified for practical reasons, while others may have been altered for unknown, illogical, or even illegal purposes. In any case, these unusual and sometimes unique firearms fall into a special class that is of interest to collectors and historians who enjoy the challenge of studying and explaining them.

As noted in chapter 1, 1965 vz. 50 serial number B66004 is unique, having been experimentally chambered for the 9 mm Browning cartridge. It is pictured by Skramouššký and Badalík (1996, 233), equipped with a vz. 70 magazine and grip panels; markings are similar to the fourth variation except that the encircled 7,65 caliber has been replaced by a 9. Unlike the earlier ČZ models 24 and 27, which share common magazines that will accept either 7.65 mm or 9 mm Browning cartridges, vz. 50-70 magazines are too narrow to accommodate 9 mm rounds, so the conversion required enlargement of the magazine body, magazine well, and breech face. Consideration was given to producing a version of the vz. 70 chambered for the 9 mm Makarov cartridge, but the difference in case diameter between 9 mm Browning (0.373") and 9 mm Makarov (0.390") would have required further modifications to handle the Soviet service round and could have thinned the chamber wall enough to raise safety concerns, probably contributing to the rejection of the proposal, although development of the design for the vz. 82 and ČZ 83 pistols may have been the deciding factor in terminating the project.

When a 62-dated vz. 50 serial numbered 20995 appeared on an internet auction site in 2008, it caught the author's attention; its date indicated that it should carry a B serial prefix and the number itself was out of sequence with other reported 61- and 62-dated vz. 50s by a factor of about 6,000, not entirely unreasonable with the normal overlapping of dates and serial numbers but still odd. It was serialized only on the receiver over the chamber, not on the slide, inconsistent with other vz. 50-70s; other markings were normal. The only way to examine the pistol in detail was to purchase it, so the author added it to his reference collection for a modest price. When it arrived, it was immediately apparent that the pistol had been altered; placing

Anomalies, Oddities, and Unique Specimens

1962-dated vz. 50 with anomalous serial number "20995" on the chamber only

a straightedge on the right side of the slide showed that about 0.5 mm of metal had been removed from the area where the serial number should have been and the right side of the chamber also showed evidence of metal removal. The sideplate contours and tool marks matched the receiver, showing it to be original, and it carried the number 950, confirming that the serial number had been altered. The lower left side of the receiver grip frame bridge carried the control number 11232, consistent with other mid-B-series vz. 50s, and the 7 in the encircled caliber designation had a central crossbar, typical of pistols in the B42000–B43000 serial range. None of the digits in the replaced serial number had stylistic features of those used at ZUB, but this type of alteration would not have been done at the factory and was probably not even done in Czechoslovakia. Under 10× magnification, traces of the first two serial numerals, 4 and 2, are visible on the chamber, and together with the sideplate number it is evident that the original serial number was B42950. Customs officers evidently considered the altered number to be illegitimate, since the pistol carries the dot-matrix import number SER. CZ5000005 on the bottom front of the receiver. Someone put a good deal of effort into changing this pistol's identity before it was imported, but for what reason? The most logical explanation is that the original serial number was removed to make it untraceable and the replacement was intended to make it appear legitimate.

Another pistol, a 1978 vz. 70, carries the neatly applied serial number "16380" in the normal position on both the slide and receiver, using 2 mm numerals. This number should have contained six digits and all observed 1978 serial numbers fall into the 400000 range, but if one assumes that the 4 is simply missing, number 416380 should have been produced in 1977. The numerals are not of the size and style used by ZUB in 1978, with the 1 having no base serif, the 3 being flat topped, and the 6 having an "open" top curve. As with "20995," the only way to examine it directly was by purchasing it and when it arrived, it was evident that the original

Czech Cold War Police Pistols 65

Chapter 5

A 1978 vz. 70 illegitimately numbered "16380"

serial numbers had been removed and replaced, rebluing the slide but leaving the chamber "white," but the work was professionally done and the numerals were evenly spaced and carefully aligned, evidently using a template or jig. The renumbering appears purposeful; like "20995," it could have been "sanitized" and renumbered to make it appear legitimate while being untraceable, but the care with which it was done suggests that it was part of a group of pistols similarly altered for sale on the black market. This raises the question of whether the renumbering was done before or after the pistol was imported and whether it is evidence of a criminal enterprise in the US. Number "16380" carries a sideplate serial number, the highest observed example, but it has been partly obliterated by buffing. It appears to be 0892, which would make 420892, 430892, 440892, 450892, 460892, 470892, and 480892 possible for the original number. The author wrote to the importer, PW Arms of Redmond, Washington, requesting information on any of these serial numbers among their records in an effort to find answers to the questions this pistol presents, but there has been no response.

Comparison of two illegitimate serial numbers; note the similarity of the 1s and 3s.

This brings us to 80-dated vz. 70 serial number "753251." As noted in chapter 2, ZUB records show that the highest vz. 70 serial number used was 724536, corresponding closely with the endpoint in the database. The date on this pistol suggests that its first serial digit should have been a 6, which would place it comfortably within the 1980 serial range near the point where the triangle prefix became standardized, and the author therefore identified it as a factory numbering error—a rare collector's prize. However, when preparing to photograph it for this book under bright lights the serial digits didn't look right; they were slightly smaller than normal, not as deeply struck, and under close examination the 3 was seen to be flat topped—a numeral style not used by ZUB.

66 The ČZ Models 50 and 70

Anomalies, Oddities, and Unique Specimens

1980 vz. 70 illegitimately numbered "753251"

The numerals were precisely spaced and the slide and receiver numbers were aligned, as if a jig had been used. When compared side by side with "16380," it was immediately apparent that the 1s and 3s had been struck with the same die; both pistols had been faked by the same person, exploding the factory error theory. The side flats of both slides showed identical fine vertical tool marks from the refinishing process (these flats are normally buffed smooth), and while it is more difficult to see, "753251" also has a slight depression where the original serial number was removed. Both pistols were imported by PW Arms and probably came from the same surplus lot, but sideplates were no longer being serialized in 1980 so there are no further clues to help identify the original serial number. The five-digit fake was easily spotted but this one was not; without the telltale 3 and the information gathered from "16830," it would probably have escaped notice. Since the author has encountered two of these fakes in just three years, there are probably many others "out there."

Vz. 70 serial number 92517, dated 74, is a CZ factory error, missing its first serial digit; based on the observed 1974 serial range it should have been numbered 192517. Unlike the three pistols discussed above, its original finish is intact with no evidence of tampering; its serial digits are correct for the period (the 1 has base serifs like numerals used in 1973, evidently applied before the old dies were replaced) and the sideplate is correctly numbered 2517 using the same dies. The numbers were neatly applied by hand, not using a jig, and the missing digit was probably the result of the worker involved simply being distracted. It evidently passed inspection and was shipped from the factory without the error being corrected; it is in excellent condition and according to the importer was part of a group of pistols acquired from a European collection. The error was not recognized; the pistol generated little interest when offered and the author purchased it for a modest price.

Another interesting anomaly is a vz. 50 offered for sale by Rock Island Auction Co. in February 2016. This pistol carries the serial number 651752 both on

Chapter 5

NB 50–marked serial number 696189 with sixteen-groove slide; note the size difference between the receiver and slide numerals and the styling of the 1s.

its receiver and slide, consistent with production at Strakonicé in 1950, but its slide has fourth-variation markings applied at ZUB and sixteen gripping grooves in the fifth-variation pattern adopted in August 1967. The pistol was equipped with the early solid, rounded hammer and showed no slide proof or date; its only visible proof was the commercial ℕ stamped over the chamber at Strakonicé. It could be examined only through photographs, and the most reasonable explanation is that its slide was damaged in the 1967–70 period and the pistol was sent in for repair, where the workshop fitted it with a new slide of the type then in production, numbered to match the receiver. RIA confirmed that the pistol's markings appeared unaltered and original; there are differences in the numeral style used on the slide, but that is not surprising.

A similar slide substitution is seen is NB 50–marked serial number 696189, also produced at Strakonicé. This pistol is also fitted with a correctly numbered fourth-variation sixteen-groove slide without proof or date; it has been retrofitted with a magazine-retaining spring and it has a vz. 70 finger rest on its original seven-hole magazine body and vz. 70 grip panels that have aged with the pistol. The slide serial digits are consistent with those used at ZUB from 1978 to 1983, but this type of repair would have been done by a contract repair shop, not the factory. The receiver carries the remnants of a ℕ proof stamped over the chamber, which was probably buffed out during refinishing since the receiver serial number and government ownership marks also show evidence of buffing. The pistol lacks import markings and thus did not enter the US through normal surplus channels; its exterior has a fair amount of service wear but its interior shows little evidence of being fired. Another pistol, vz. 70 serial number 244872 (not pictured), which would be expected to have been produced in 1975–76, also carries no slide proof or date and probably has a replaced slide.

Vz. 70 serial number D86192 (not pictured) has special modifications for use with a silencer, including an extended, threaded barrel and an elevated sight rib to make the sights usable with the silencer installed. It carries no date, type, or national-origin markings and was rumored to have been prepared for Venezuelan terrorist Ilich Ramirez Sanchez ("Carlos the Jackal"), sentenced to two life prison terms in France for murders committed in the 1970s. The National Automatic Pistol Collectors Association (NAPCA) reviewed a similar pistol, with photos by Otto Matyska, in the March 2017 issue of its publication *Automag*, noting that 110 of these pistols were produced and that the one pictured, with silencer, is in the national crime lab in the Czech Republic. While interesting, the "Jackal" story has never been validated and Sanchez was known to have favored pistols chambered for the 7.62 × 25 mm cartridge, casting doubt on the connection. At least one vz. 70, serial number 117637, has an extended, threaded barrel for use with a silencer but lacks the other unusual features described above; whether this was factory work or a later modification is not known.

58-dated vz. 50 serial number B17890 is equipped with a 105 mm barrel, extending 12 mm beyond the front of the slide and evidently intended to allow attachment of a silencer, as there is no other logical explanation for it. The barrel is not threaded so the silencer would require a clamping collet for attachment; its exposed front shows wear marks consistent with use of such a device. The muzzle is not crowned to provide a better gas seal in a clamping collet. Serial number B21219, also dated 58, has a similar extended barrel but has not been examined by the author. No information is available on the silencers that were used with these pistols, but those made for the ČZ model 27 during World War II had a six-finger clamping collet and were 35 mm in diameter and 203 mm long; it can be assumed that a similar type was made for the vz. 50. (The silenced ČZ 27 had an extended barrel with a larger diameter slotted front end that engaged a lug on the silencer to align its auxiliary sights; this was not feasible with the vz. 50's fixed barrel and concentric recoil spring.) The number of these pistols produced is unknown, probably not more than 100, and they are clearly rare. Old Western Scrounger reported that this pistol was imported from Bosnia-Hercegovina, formerly part of Yugoslavia, in 2020; it displays significant finish loss, surface freckling, and light pitting from extensive use and had heavy interior wear that required major parts replacement to function properly. A damaged magazine and grip panels were replaced before the photo was taken.

Two 72-dated vz. 70s without the national-origin line in their slide legends have been pictured on the I.pinimg.com website, one with a hole drilled through its lower rear grip panels, presumably to accommodate a lanyard. Photos of the pistols' right sides had the serial number blurred out, making further identification impossible. They may have been prepared for clandestine use, but the author has never seen one offered for sale and has thus had no opportunity to purchase and examine one.

Vz. 50 serial number 676273 has a small, round, dome-like protrusion on the top of the slide rib, just forward of the rear sight, 4.5 mm in diameter and 0.020" high. It is directly above the firing-pin lock recess, and the sectional drawing (page 103) shows only a thin layer of steel at that point, about 0.5 mm thick. The probable explanation is that the boring tool for the lock recess was replaced just before the pistol's slide went through that machining process and

Bulge above the firing-pin lock on the slide of vz. 50 serial number 676273

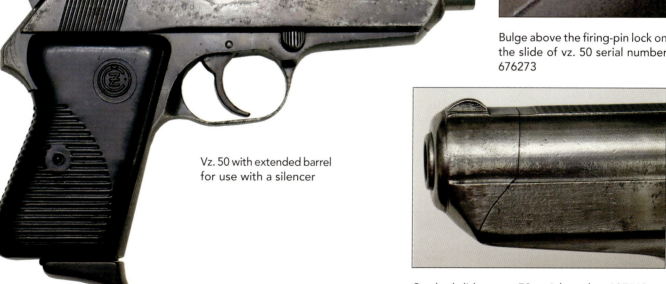

Vz. 50 with extended barrel for use with a silencer

Cracked slide on vz. 70 serial number 105160

Chapter 5

NB 50–marked serial number 659090 and 1970 vz. 50 serial number D67329 are fitted with aluminum grip panels.

its setting was a little too deep, but the heat generated by the operation caused the steel to flex rather than rupturing, leaving the dome as it cooled. It would be interesting to know whether the tool setting was immediately corrected or the problem persisted, but the randomization created during further machining operations would scatter any other examples over a fairly wide serial range, making them very difficult to locate and identify.

Anomalies, Oddities, and Unique Specimens

The "fifth pair" of aluminum grips, evidently made from a different mold; note small voids

Vz. 70 serial number 105160, dated 72, has a crack in the left side of its slide extending from the lower front corner diagonally upward to a point about 9 mm behind the front sight, across the sighting rib, and 5 mm down the right side, evidently caused by impact of the interior front lug against the disassembly button during recoil. Cracked slides are occasionally encountered in vz. 52 army pistols due to stress from their high-pressure cartridge and locking system, but they are highly unusual in pistols chambered for the relatively mild .32 ACP round. Interior wear points on number 105160 do not indicate excessive service use, suggesting that the crack was the result of firing overloaded cartridges. Before the pistol was imported, it was sprayed with a black polymer coating that resists normal paint-stripping chemicals, probably to hide the damage and effectively immobilizing parts such as the extractor and cartridge indicator. The dealer from whom the author bought it removed some of the coating, discovered the crack, and sold it as a "parts only" gun for a modest price. It could be restored to shooting status by replacing the slide but the author chose to retain it, with the firing pin and lock removed for safety, as a cautionary example of the risks of disregarding ammunition-reloading guidelines. Firing the pistol in its current condition could extend the crack, allowing the front of the slide to separate and the remainder to be driven forcefully off the receiver toward the shooter, possibly causing serious injury. Could it be repaired? Yes, by milling out the entire length of the crack, welding it together, reshaping the weld to match normal contours, engraving the sighting rib to restore the stamped wave pattern, and rebluing the entire pistol. This might be a worthwhile project for a novice or apprentice gunsmith developing practical skills, but it would otherwise be a waste of professional time.

Four known vz. 50s are equipped with cast aluminum (or aluminum alloy) grip panels, NB 50– marked serial numbers 659090, 659233, and 659247 and 70-dated serial number D67329. Czech sources state that ČZ did not produce aluminum panels for these pistols, although the clustering of the three NB 50 serial numbers strongly suggests a relationship; they were probably drawn from the same storage case. These grip panels were evidently cast in the same molds; markings on their inner faces are blurred but mirror those on original Strakonicé panels, indicating that the molds were made from that type. None of these pistols is import-marked, consistent with GI "bring-back" weapons from a war zone; three of the four are in nearly new condition and came without provenance information, while the fourth, number 659090, has been refinished to hide extensive surface pitting, has a bore nearly destroyed by the use of corrosive-primed ammunition without proper cleaning, and was claimed to have been captured in 1969 by a GI serving in Vietnam, although no documentation was provided. A fifth pair of the panels, also painted black, was purchased by the author from a parts dealer who said that it had come from a pistol confiscated and decommissioned by police. There was no record of its serial number but the seller thought it had been taken from a Vietnam veteran. This pair of panels was apparently cast from a different mold based on originals used by ZUB, since inside surfaces show no subcontractor markings; they have several small voids that do not affect serviceability but suggest that they were produced later and with less care, perhaps to repair pistols issued with Bakelite grips that had been damaged. It is also possible that they were used on vz. 70s, although no vz. 70 with aluminum grips has been observed.

Recently discovered serial number D67306, evidently also a Vietnam GI "bring-back," is identical to D67329 except that it retains its original Bakelite grips. However, its right panel has a feature unique to very late production vz. 50s, a hammer pivot recess that is round rather than hexagonal, also found on the "fifth pair" of aluminum panels. Given the very rough exterior of D67329's grips, it is probable that the molds used to make them were worn out and had to be discarded, using the Bakelite panels removed from D67329 or another pistol in the lot to make the new set of molds used for the "fifth pair," and D67306 was shipped out while the new molds were being made.

Czech Cold War Police Pistols 71

Chapter 5

NB 52–marked serial number 733662 with modified hammer and polished chamber, hammer, and trigger

At the beginning of US military involvement in Vietnam, North Vietnamese troops were armed with World War II–era French, US, and Japanese weapons, plus a mixture of other military surplus material. The country had no appreciable arms industry before 1975 but was supplied with weapons and ammunition by Communist China and several Warsaw Pact nations; US troops serving there encountered Czech vz. 50 and 52 pistols as well as vz. 61 Škorpion machine pistols. The Bakelite grips on vz. 50s are easily broken when impacted or dropped and while the resulting damage is often minor, fractures in the butt area can leave the pistol difficult to aim and fire, as the Vietnamese had probably learned from combat experience. The author's theory is that in response to such damage, North Vietnam produced molds to cast replacement grips, using aluminum for added strength. The standard North Vietnamese army sidearm was the Chinese type 54, a copy of the Soviet TT33 Tokarev, so smaller, more easily concealed pistols such as the vz. 50 were probably supplied to the Viet Cong, a clandestine Communist political and paramilitary force that operated in South Vietnam with support from the North. The three Strakonice pistols were probably shipped to North Vietnam in the mid-1960s when US involvement escalated following the Tonkin Gulf Incident and were modified and sent to Viet Cong units in the South. Serial number 659090 evidently reached its destination and saw extensive jungle warfare before being captured, while numbers 659233 and 659247 were probably intercepted and captured en route. Serial number D67329 was produced about a month before the vz. 70 model change and was probably part of another small lot of pistols shipped to North Vietnam and fitted with aluminum panels. This lot would not have reached South Vietnam before 1971 and by that time US troops were being drawn down, reducing their chances of encountering them, but the condition of D67329 suggests that it was also intercepted before reaching the Viet Cong and went home in a GI's duffel bag.

Although this theory involves a good deal of speculation, it is completely plausible; the Vietnam War, with extensions into Cambodia and Laos, was the only US military engagement lasting from the mid-1960s to the mid-1970s that provided GIs the opportunity to capture and bring home weapons of this type. Communist China, the supplier of most North Vietnamese ammunition, was one of the few manufacturers still using corrosive priming through the 1970s, explaining the condition of number

Anomalies, Oddities, and Unique Specimens

"Transitional" vz. 70 serial number D78512; note vz. 50 receiver contours, polished chamber, and improvised lanyard loop.

659390's bore, but it is unlikely that China would have undertaken a small project such as the aluminum grip panel fabrication and retained the molds in anticipation of a follow-up order. The idea has been advanced that the panels were produced for aircraft use, but since a pair of aluminum panels weigh twice as much as the original Bakelite panels (102 g vs. 51 g), this is illogical. The theory will remain unproven unless documentation surfaces verifying Vietnam War capture of such pistols or the casting of aluminum grips by the former North Vietnamese government.

NB 52–marked serial number 733662 is equipped with the standard hammer used on vz. 50s manufactured before mid-1967 but it has a chamfered 4 mm diameter transverse hole drilled through the spur, similar to the 5 mm diameter holes in the hammers of vz. 52 army pistols. The hammer is polished "white," as are the trigger, barrel, and chamber visible through the ejection port, perhaps to make the pistol stand out, distinguishing it from others. When first examined, it was thought that it might have been a "trial gun" for the ring hammer adopted in 1967—and this is a plausible explanation—but it assumes that the hole itself was a desirable feature, perhaps to assist in manual decocking, not a weight-reducing compensation for the ring hammer's larger size. The pistol could also have been modified by a previous owner to personalize it, which is a more logical explanation. Its interior shows evidence of extensive firing but it has been well maintained, with only light, uniform wear on its exterior finish.

As noted in chapter 2, the four lowest-numbered known vz. 70s, D78266, D78308, D78427, and D78512, are transitional, consisting of vz. 70 slides, grip panels, and magazines assembled on matching-numbered vz. 50 receivers that lack the revised contours described in chapter 3. When the first of these appeared (the one pictured here), it was thought to be an anomaly, but the discovery of three additional specimens demonstrates that they represent a transitional variant for which numbers can only be roughly estimated from the data currently available. Number D78308 was imported by Century Arms International in 2020 and came without provenance information. D78266 and D78427 were imported by PW Arms of Redmond, Washington, probably as part of a large lot of Czech municipal police trade-ins that they purchased in 2010–2011 and ended up in a group of twenty-one "gunsmith specials" sold by Classic Arms. Number D78512 was part of a small lot of Israeli police trade-ins imported by Mach 1 Arsenal of Knoxville, Tennessee

Czech Cold War Police Pistols

in 2015, with polished chambers and improvised lanyard loops made by drilling a 2.5 mm diameter hole through the lower right rear of the grip frame, cutting a corresponding notch in the right grip panel, and inserting a 12 mm split ring. The Israelis also polished the receiver-slide bearing surfaces, giving the pistol unusually smooth cycling, and finished the job by rebluing it, since the spot of red paint is missing from the safety indicator recess and slide markings lack normal edge "cratering." At the time this pistol was produced, the Czech government was not on friendly terms with Israel and the purchase was probably arranged through an intermediary. If the grouping of the transitional variant serial numbers was consistent it would suggest that they represent a block of more than two hundred similar pistols, but as can be seen from table 2-3, vz. 50 serial number D78340 interrupts the series, demonstrating that such a conclusion would be incorrect. We do not know the ratio of vz. 50s to vz. 70s occupying the data gaps or whether additional specimens will be clustered or scattered; we also do not know how far below number D78266 or how far above D78512 the transitional range may extend. However, it appears that a significant number of transitional pistols were assembled and it would be prudent to carefully examine any pistol encountered from the D78000 serial block to ascertain its identity. Regardless of the conclusion, the data would be valuable to better document the transition period.

Vz. 50 serial number D77646 (not pictured), a pistol that falls very close to the vz. 70 transition period, is equipped with a vz. 70 magazine and grip panels that are probably original, based on the pistol's condition. It shows only light finish wear around the muzzle and a small spot of ring finger wear on the front grip strap, mirroring the condition of the panels. It is therefore assumed to be an example of overlapping, assembled out of order after the vz. 70 parts had been integrated into the assembly process. Serial number D72703 is not as close to the model change but also carries a vz. 70 magazine and grip panels and shows little evidence of use. While it is impossible to verify these pistols' originality, they provide an interesting view of conditions that may have prevailed at ZUB around the change period, when the focus was evidently on closing out the old model and sending the new one to market.

Vz. 50 serial number D68703, proof-dated 79

Anomalies, Oddities, and Unique Specimens

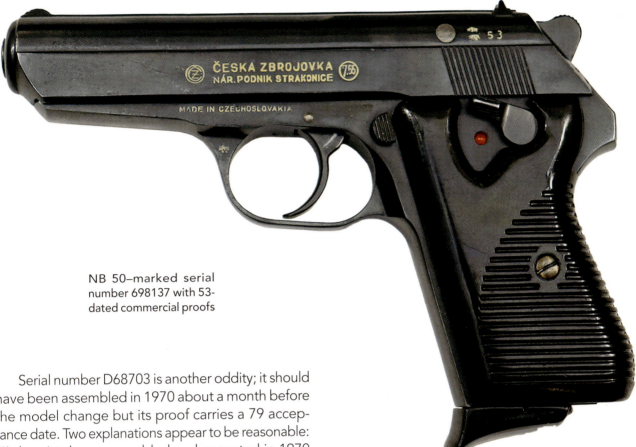

NB 50–marked serial number 698137 with 53-dated commercial proofs

Serial number D68703 is another oddity; it should have been assembled in 1970 about a month before the model change but its proof carries a 79 acceptance date. Two explanations appear to be reasonable: (1) the pistol was assembled and accepted in 1970 but the worker who proofed it picked up the wrong numeral die when applying the date, or (2) it was misplaced or held back for nine years before being completed and accepted. The first explanation is implausible because, as noted in chapter 3, ZUB used two-digit date stamps, so the worker responsible for stamping the proof mark and date on the pistol's slide would have no reason for other dies to be on his workbench. The second could have resulted from the incomplete pistol being lost and later rediscovered—also implausible—or from its rejection due to a defect or mechanical problem, causing it to be shelved for later readjustment and acceptance. One can assume that if it had been accepted and incorrectly dated in 1970 it would have been fitted with a vz. 50 magazine and grip panels, while if completed in 1979 it would have been assembled with the components then in use. Unfortunately, it had after-market replacement grip panels and came from a collector's estate; the heir searched for its original panels at the author's request, but found nothing. The pistol had a vz. 70 magazine but magazines are interchangeable, leaving the question temporarily moot. After purchasing it, the author found that its sideplate had been replaced; it did not match the receiver contours and had been removed from a vz. 70 with the last four serial digits 7913. The hold-open catch was not the type used in 1970 but was the later type adopted in 1976, with the receiver modified to accommodate it before it was finished, validating the 79 acceptance date; the author therefore restored it with vz. 70 grip panels. It was evidently involved in the 1979–82 rebuilding program and it is somewhat surprising that other examples of pistols rejected and later rebuilt have not surfaced.

Rare dates are always of interest to collectors; few vz. 50-70s were produced in 1957, 1963, and 1983, making them desirable, and vz. 50s from 1960 are also scarce. Since there was no vz. 50 production from 1953 to 1956 these dates should be impossible to find, but the author owns or has observed vz. 50s

Stripped, poor-condition vz. 70 slide serial number 127896, proof dated 79 over 72

Czech Cold War Police Pistols 75

Chapter 5

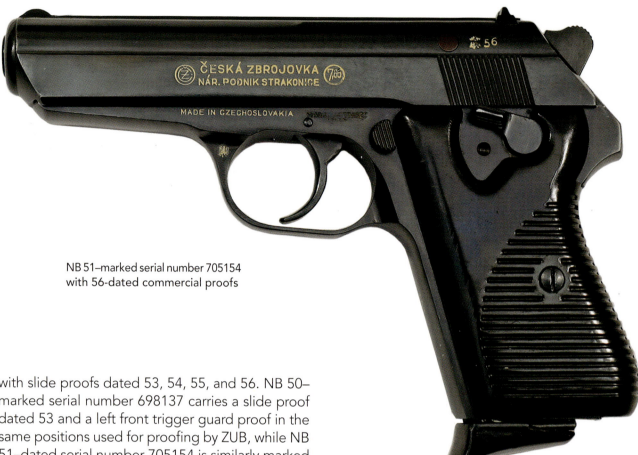

NB 51–marked serial number 705154 with 56-dated commercial proofs

with slide proofs dated 53, 54, 55, and 56. NB 50–marked serial number 698137 carries a slide proof dated 53 and a left front trigger guard proof in the same positions used for proofing by ZUB, while NB 51–dated serial number 705154 is similarly marked with a 56 proof date. Since proofing is done to test the strength of the barrel reproofing would logically be done only if the barrel was replaced, but both of these pistols appear to be in nearly unissued condition—why replace their barrels? The answer is actually fairly simple; while the quality of factory ammunition has improved significantly over the past few decades, in the 1950s both standards and the sophistication of loading machinery were not as high, particularly in countries under Communist rule. The most common defect in ammunition manufacturing is a missing or inadequate powder charge, producing a "squib" load that will usually propel the bullet from the case mouth into the barrel but may leave it lodged there, while forcing the breech to open far enough to vent primer and powder gas. An inexperienced shooter encountering this problem and wondering why his pistol didn't function properly is likely to manually cycle the slide, ejecting the empty cartridge case and chambering a fresh round, and attempt to fire again. Firing a second round with a bullet lodged in the bore will propel both bullets from the barrel, but the excess pressure generated will "ring" the barrel, leaving a stretched spot that will impair accuracy and may prevent the slide from cycling, requiring the pistol to be repaired. With this, and the proof and date locations being identical to those used by ZUB in mind, the author assumed that the leftover parts inventory from Strakonicé had been sent to ZUB, and any needed repairs would have been handled there, but in discussing these odd-dated pistols with David Pazdera he learned that ZUB had nothing to do with vz. 50s before 1957 and had to restart production from the ground up at that time; leftover parts from Strakonicé would have gone to workshops and arms repair companies that handled such matters for the government and would have rebarreled these pistols. This creates a small class of unusual redated pistols; thirty-five are recorded in the database from Strakonicé and four from ZUB, carrying reproofing dates ranging from 53 to 81. In cases where a dated proof was already stamped on the slide, overstamping the date was apparently acceptable; vz 50 serial numbers D68776 and D68972 and vz. 70 serial numbers J62534 and 127890 are examples. The latter pistol was evidently allowed to deteriorate and was then sold for parts, but it had been reproofed, and its slide is stamped 79 over 72. (The reason for the much-larger number of known

Anomalies, Oddities, and Unique Specimens

NB 51–marked serial number 707141 with double Ⓣ proofs

reproofed Strakonicé pistols than from ZUB is that the majority of the early production vz. 50s remained in Czechoslovakia and were repaired there as needed, while most of the vz. 50-70s from ZUB were exported and would not have been repaired by Czech workshops. Serial numbers D68776, D68972, J62534, and 127890 were probably allocated to Czech municipal police departments.)

NB 51–marked vz. 50 serial number 707141 carries two Strakonicé factory Ⓣ proofs over the chamber but no slide proof and date, suggesting that it might have been damaged and subsequently rebarreled and reproofed by the factory, but information provided by David Pazdera indicates that factory operations were organized around production, not repair, and would not have accepted a damaged pistol for rebarreling. Could a distracted or absent-minded factory worker simply have stamped the chamber twice by mistake? Apparently not, since the two proofs were stamped by dies of slightly different sizes, indicating that it probably was actually proofed twice. This defies logical explanation but it clearly makes the pistol a unique and interesting specimen.

Vz. 50 serial number 728834 is an example of one of the more difficult vz. 50-70 variants for US collectors to find, a 1952 commercial. It is in excellent condition with little evidence of internal wear but it also has been reproofed, with a 67 date and the proof sequence number 4501, indicating that it was handled by the independent Czech proofing house in Prague, not a repair workshop. Considering that virtually all the Strakonicé-produced commercial vz. 50s were exported, this pistol was evidently reimported in 1967 and import regulations required it to be reproofed. It is certainly an unusual specimen. NB 50–marked serial number 684787 (not pictured) was evidently reimported in 1992 and is stamped ·7567·92·🛡 on the left side of the slide forward of the gripping grooves.

One 69-dated vz. 50 (not pictured but posted on an internet site), serial numbered 220545, is clearly an error. It has sixteen slide grooves and is equipped with a large-hole ring hammer and grooved

1952 commercial serial number 728834 with added 67-dated commercial proof and proof sequence number

Czech Cold War Police Pistols

Chapter 5

71-dated vz. 70 "4968" with defaced serial number, added inscription, and smooth disassembly button. *Alan J. Bell collection and photo*

takedown button, correct for a C-series pistol, but its acceptance date should place its serial number above C62000, making both its first and second digits incorrect. The slide and receiver numbers match and the sideplate is numbered 0545, providing no clues to further identify it, but C70545, C80545, and C90545 would be logical candidates for its proper number. It has postproduction nickel plating, but in the author's opinion it would have been more interesting with its original finish intact.

Perhaps the strangest anomaly the author has seen is 71-dated vz. 70 serial number "4968." It appears that a rotary-milling cutter was used to remove the letter prefix and first serial digit both from the receiver and slide numbers, leaving donut-shaped impressions that are approximately 8 mm in diameter and 2 mm deep. The pistol was then reblued and the inscription "TOMAŠU OD O U P—a 1989" was engraved on the right front of the slide. The inscription is not written in proper Czech—possibly a Moravian dialect (Jan Balcar, personal communication)—but it appears to signify that the pistol was presented by "Thomas" to a person or organization identified as "O U P," possibly a government unit, in 1989. (The Czech *a* is normally a conjunction meaning "and" or "plus," but in this dialect it probably identified 1989 as a date rather than an organization number, but since vz. 70 production ended in 1983, it could have had a different meaning.) The pistol is equipped with the early type of hammer pivot, and that, combined with its acceptance date, places it between serial numbers D85000 and J16538, making D94968, J04968, and J14968 viable candidates. It is equipped with a flat disassembly button without checkering, evidently an incompletely machined factory part; this suggests a factory connection, and since ZUB is located in southeastern Moravia, the use of a Moravian dialect by a factory worker is completely plausible. It is uncertain whether the cutout over the chamber is deep enough to make this pistol unsafe to fire and the reason for defacing a "presentation" pistol in this way defies logical

Vz. 50 Sport pistol, field stripped

Anomalies, Oddities, and Unique Specimens

NB 52 marked vz. 50 Sport pistol serial number 710608, rebuilt in 1963

Vz. 50 Sport pistol rear sight

explanation unless it had *already* been defaced and was being presented as some sort of symbol or prank. In 2021, Old Western Scrounger LLC (ows-ammo.com) offered a number of vz. 70s for sale as "parts guns" that had their slides and chambers drilled through in the same positions (removing the first part of the serial numbers) with similar but deeper tool holes, evidently to deface their serial numbers and to deactivate them, so that was probably the intent with "4968." A request to Old Western Scrounger for import information on these pistols' import origin generated no response.

As noted in chapter 2, in 1963 a significant number of vz. 50s produced at Strakonicé for the MV were withdrawn from storage and sent to the

Czech Cold War Police Pistols

Lovena workshop for modification into "Sport" pistols for export sale. Production may have extended into 1964, but the author has been unable to document this; it probably ended when the factory was again able to satisfy export needs. Serial number 731571 carries the West German import marks of Waffen Frankonia Würzberg and was offered for sale on the Czech internet outlet Panzer.cz for 16,000 Kč (about US $600) in 2019. Serial number 722328, dated 63, is reported to be in the US, although no details are available. Serial number 762152, also dated 63, was imported by DWJ Imports in 2022 and sold for $750 but received only one bid. Two of these pistols, NB 52–marked serial numbers 719608 and 727317, were imported by Century Arms International in 2011 and sold to a resident of Idaho; in 2019, they were again offered for sale on GunBroker.com for about $500 each and were purchased by the author for study and evaluation. Modifications included removal of the original sights and barrel; installation of a new 150 mm barrel with a square-profile 2 mm wide front sight pinned to a sleeve mounted on it, retained by a knurled nut threaded onto the muzzle to allow disassembly for cleaning and maintenance; and mounting of a new rear sight on a frame extension welded to the rear grip tang and machined to match the original frame contours. This gave the pistol a length of 270 mm (10⅝"), a weight of 826 g, and a sight radius of 220 mm, compared to 127 mm in the original vz. 50. The front sight base has an indexing lug stamped in its bottom that engages a groove in the barrel to ensure proper alignment. The rear sight has a 2.5 mm wide U-shaped notch and is mounted on a vertically sliding plate secured to the frame extension with two screws, allowing it to be adjusted for elevation; five horizontal index lines are stamped on the left side of the rear sight base, with a single zeroing line opposing them on the left side of the sight. (Both of the author's specimens came with the zero aligned with the lowest index line, correct for a range of 25 m.) A transverse windage adjustment screw is also provided. The author's specimens came equipped with reduced-tension hammer springs, probably installed by the previous owner; this reduces trigger pull weight, improving potential accuracy, but the replacement springs will not ignite primers reliably from the shorter double-action hammer stroke, effectively converting the pistols to single-action-only firing. Number 719608 had mechanical issues when

received, with a heavily worn hammer and sear that would not function in the double-action mode, but it also had an overtightened hammer pivot nut that squeezed the sideplate against the firing mechanism, preventing the trigger bar from resetting behind the sear after firing. Both of the author's sport pistols have Czech commercial proofs stamped on the chamber below the original Ⓣ proof, on the left side of the slide forward of the gripping grooves, and on the upper left front of the trigger guard; the slide proofs are dated 63 (all observed specimens have 63 proof dates, although Czech sources identify them only as being "rebuilt in the first half of the 1960s"). The extended sight radius, improved sight picture, removal of the influence of lateral slide play, and increased weight all contribute to improved accuracy. When fired from a sandbag rest at 25 m, the author's specimens produced somewhat tighter groups than an unmodified Strakonicé vz. 50, but the author's vision is becoming compromised by advancing age and a younger shooter could probably produce more-definitive results. The rear sight extension makes disassembly and manual cycling of the slide somewhat awkward and the cost of .32 ACP ammunition, compared to .22 Long Rifle cartridges, makes them relatively expensive for plinking and target use. Internet "chatter" suggests that there are at least a few more of these pistols in the US, but no further data have been provided on them.

There are two vz. 50 factory cutaway pistols in the collection of the Czech Army Museum in Prague, although they may actually have been prepared by a contracting workshop rather than the Strakonicé factory itself (the Czechs refer to these pistols as *řez*, "cut," or *školní řez*, "school cut"). Serial number 710477 was produced at Strakonicé in 1951 but it was either sectioned or updated in 1970 or later, since it is equipped with the small-hole ring hammer; a flat, checkered disassembly button; and a vz. 70 magazine and grip panels. The second cutaway is not serial numbered and has the early solid hammer, grooved disassembly button, and a vz. 50 magazine and grip panels. Two cutaway pistols, 1952 vz. 50 serial number 727978 and an unserialized vz. 70, have been offered on the internet site Armybazar. eu (Czech Republic), but no further details are available. Metal removal patterns on 727978 are similar to the two museum specimens, but the unserialized vz. 70 has considerably smaller cutouts on the sideplate and is equipped with a ring hammer, checkered

Anomalies, Oddities, and Unique Specimens

Vz. 70 factory cutaway serial number X2001

disassembly button, and vz. 70 grip panels and magazine. Another vz. 50 cutaway, serial number C20607, was offered on Armyburza.cz, presumably a different address for the same organization, with vz. 70 small parts, grips, and sectioned magazine. Viewing ports on the vz. 50 cutaways show the right side of the firing mechanism, the magazine, the firing pin and its lock, the hammer spring and strut, the interior of the chamber, and the recoil spring and barrel interior. Serial number 710477 is blued, while the other pistols have nickel-plated receivers and slides, although other parts are blued; the unserialized museum pistol's hammer spring and hammer pivot nut are missing. It is quite possible that other vz. 50 cutaways will appear. Another pair of cutaway pistols, vz. 50 serial number D75857 and vz. 70 serial number 187275, were pictured in a Czech internet estate auction; both were nickel plated, had vz. 70 grip panels and sectioned magazines, and were probably prepared by the same workshop that produced number C20607, noted above, on the basis of cutting patterns. A number of these pistols were probably converted for training purposes.

Two vz. 70 factory cutaway pistols are also known, although a third without a serial number has been offered for sale on an international auction site and at least as many as ten were probably produced; machinists' drawings for them are located in the ZUB archives (David Pazdera, personal communication). Both known pistols were imported by Century Arms International in the first few years of the 2000s, where they languished in a display case for more than a decade before being "rediscovered" in 2019 and offered for sale on the internet. They have extensive finish wear on the front grip strap and slide-gripping area, were missing small parts, and had evidently been used for training, probably by the Czech MV. They are not serial-numbered in the normal position; the author's specimen carries the number X2001 on the left side of the receiver in 3 mm characters of the style used at ZUB from 1978 to 1983. The second specimen has no corresponding number but has a dot-matrix **10** stamped on the right side of the receiver, to the rear of the disassembly button (probably by the importer), and the dot-matrix marking **SER.10DUP** stamped on the front grip strap, apparently because BATFE was not satisfied with the first **10**. (The absence of similar importer-applied markings on number X2001 suggests that it was serial-numbered by the Czechs prior to export, but this is unconfirmed.) The cutaway pistols have remnants of fifth-variation markings on

US-made plastic model of the vz. 50

their slides; they are not dated but are fitted with the revised hold-open catch, indicating production in or after 1976, probably in 1978 when a large number of vz. 70s were allocated to the MV. Unlike the vz. 50 cutaways, they are sectioned on both sides of the receiver and slide. The right-side viewing ports expose the chamber interior and the interactions between the hammer, trigger bar, and sear; the magazine and magazine catch; the trigger spring and trigger bar; the firing pin and its lock; and the extractor and cartridge indicator. The left-side viewing ports expose the safety and sear bar interaction (with part of the safety removed to show the decocking mechanism), the hammer and hammer strut connection, the hold-open catch, the breech face with a cut into the rear of the chamber to show the cartridge rim and extractor groove, the recoil spring and barrel interior, and the magazine contact with its retainer spring. The magazines are not sectioned but may not be original to the pistols since it appears that they had been partially cannibalized for parts. The author replaced the firing pin (with its tip removed for safety), the firing-pin lock and spring, the trigger spring, and the hammer pivot nut to restore number X2001. The slide-viewing ports make manual operation difficult and can pinch the operator's hand when the slide closes; the author found the use of a leather glove to be advisable during operation. In addition to being collectors' items, these cutaway pistols are excellent tools for studying and understanding nuances of the vz. 50-70's mechanism; in terms of displaying mechanical operation, they are the best-executed factory cutaways the author has examined.

Cast plastic models of the vz. 50 were produced by the US government during the Cold War era for identification and training purposes. While the models were crudely executed, their details were replicated accurately enough to identify the pistol used to produce the mold as 1950 commercial serial number 664385. In addition to being a historical curio, the model is useful for stretching tight holsters, since it is impervious to the moisture needed to soften the leather.

Vz. 69 prototype; note modified safety lever. *Česká zbrojovka a. s. factory collection, photo by David Pazdera*

Chapter 5

As noted in chapter 2, the prototype for the vz. 70 was developed at ZUB as the vz. 69. Little is known about these pistols—even their existence was unknown in the US until recently—but they clearly merit further study. The number produced and their serial range have not been released, but on the basis of the ZUB vz. 50 trial pistols, there were probably about thirty of them. One specimen is retained in the factory collection; the others are believed to be in private collections in the Czech Republic. The factory specimen is not proofed; it has no grip screw or magazine, which seems odd, considering the abundance of spare parts available. It has the small-hole ring hammer adopted in early 1970 and an unusual safety lever that has a raised rib extending from the edge of the body down and to the rear across the flat, the same type used on the Kompactní vz. 50-70. The modified safety lever was not carried forward into regular production, probably because it was more expensive to fabricate and did not significantly improve the pistol's handling quality. The vz. 69 was used as the model for the illustrations on the early vz. 70 pistol box; the publicity department at ZUB had no photographic equipment at that time (David Pazdera, personal communication), so the illustrations on boxes and instruction manuals were artist's renderings, although Omnipol promotional materials used some photos. The pistol's left side was used on the early box; no type markings are included, but the illustration shows the same revised contours, small-hole hammer, modified safety lever, magazine base, and grip panels, although the grip screw was inadvertently omitted in the drawing. The safety lever is particularly interesting because once the tooling was set up, it would be logical to fabricate enough of them not only to equip the trial pistols, but perhaps to start production on the new model. Were some of these safeties, like the extra spur hammers from the original vz. 50 prototype, mixed into the regular parts stream and used on standard production pistols? None have been observed to date, but their existence is possible and would create another interesting variant.

Also noted in chapter 2, at about the same time that the vz. 69 prototypes were produced, a Kompactní (compact) version of the vz. 50 was being developed, with several unusual features, including the vz. 69's modified safety and a completely redesigned takedown mechanism using a flanged pull-down latch installed on the inside front of the trigger guard, retained by a screw in the upper front face of the guard. Unlike the standard takedown button, it is detent-controlled, not spring-loaded, and does not require continual finger pressure while removing the slide. The pistol's slide is marked "CZ 50 32-27" on its right side, probably referencing the project number. Like the vz. 69, several of these pistols may have been assembled for testing and evaluation but their numbers and ultimate distribution have not been released. Plans to move this pistol into production as the vz. 80 were probably canceled due to the development of the military vz. 82 and commercial ČZ 83, which replaced the vz. 70.

The early vz. 70 box was not introduced until April 1971 and its use was discontinued in January 1972, apparently because the modified safety created an inaccurate depiction of the pistol and it was feared that this might negatively affect sales. A second vz. 70 box was developed, using the right side of the pistol for its cover illustration (also used on the vz. 70 instruction manual), but it was not introduced until late 1974. Its illustration also has problems, although not as obvious as those noted above; the grip screw is pictured as being inserted from the right side and the disassembly button is shown with a flat face and four horizontal grooves. It is likely that the flat, horizontally grooved button was in the planning stage when the illustration was produced and its face was changed to stamped checkering before any of the new parts were fabricated, but it is also possible that some flat, grooved buttons were made and used on production pistols before the final configuration was adopted. The disassembly button change from arched to flat

Illustration from vz. 70 manual showing a flat, horizontally grooved disassembly button

Anomalies, Oddities, and Unique Specimens

Kompaktní prototype. Česká zbrojovka a. s. factory collection, photo by David Pazdera

Czech Cold War Police Pistols

85

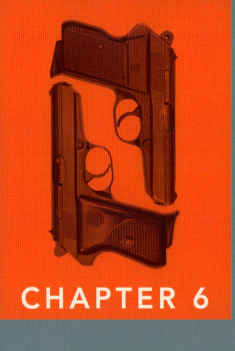

CHAPTER 6

Operational Features

Czech vz. 50-70s are unlocked breech, straight-blowback-operated semiautomatic pistols and a detailed discussion of their cycle of operation would be pointless in view of the large number of similar weapons that are familiar to firearms enthusiasts. However, their unique characteristics deserve description to aid in operation, maintenance, and repair. In order to avoid infringing on existing patents, the Kratochvíl brothers designed the new pistol almost from the ground up and their ingenuity is reflected in its operation.

Firing Mechanism

Although the parts of the mechanism are complex, the double-action system is elegant in its simplicity. The sear is 7.5 mm wide, rotating around a horizontal pin that passes through its upper rear, anchored in the receiver on the left and the sideplate on the right. Its spring is mounted in a slot in its top, wrapping around the sear pin with its left end seated against the receiver bridge forming the rear of the magazine well and its right end having a 90-degree bend that extends across the top of the sear,

Hammer, left and right sides, viewed from below. The narrow notch at bottom center is the double-action notch; the broad one to the rear is the single-action setup notch.

Sear, viewed from right rear: *left*, in new condition; *right*, with broken spur, removed from vz. 50 serial number B69414

Trigger bar, viewed from the left

88   The ČZ Models 50 and 70

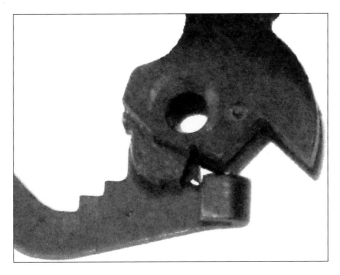

"Inside" view of contact between trigger bar stirrup and double-action notch on hammer at the initiation of double-action firing

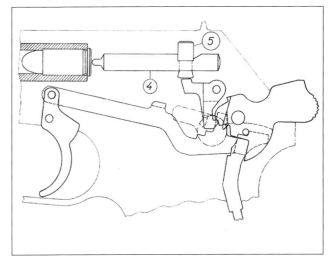

Firing mechanism, cocked, with the firing pin locked. *4*, firing pin; *5*, firing pin lock. *From first ČZ manual*

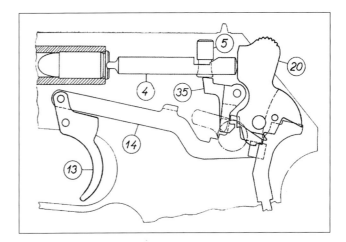

Firing mechanism an instant before firing, with the firing pin in the process of unlocking as it is struck by the hammer. *4*, firing pin; *5*, firing-pin lock; *13*, trigger; *14*, trigger bar; *20*, hammer; *35*, sear. *From first ČZ instruction manual*

pressing downward on its front. A horizontal arm on the front of the sear rides in a groove at the top of the receiver bridge, limiting its downward movement, and it interacts with the firing-pin lock; a rearward-facing spur at the bottom of the sear fits inside the safety body and interacts with the hammer and safety; and an activating lug on the right side of the sear extends 5 mm into an opening in the sideplate and interacts with the trigger bar, which passes through a recess in its bottom. The bottom of the hammer is machined to form three sectors, each with different functions. The right sector rotates and releases the hammer in the double-action mode and sets the trigger bar for single-action firing; the center sector holds and releases the hammer during single-action firing, controls the sear during double-action firing, and interacts with the hammer strut; and the left sector interacts with the safety to prevent the hammer from striking the firing pin during decocking. A safety step at the front of the hammer, bridging the right and center sectors, prevents it from contacting the firing pin when at rest. The trigger bar is 77 mm long, with a U-shaped stirrup at its rear end formed by a 180-degree lateral bend that operates the hammer in double-action firing. Forward of the stirrup, an upward-projecting spur interacts with the operation lug on the sear during single-action firing; forward of the spur there is a downward-curving section with a locking notch for the safety lug; forward of that is the disconnector cam, which interacts with the slide; and a hole at its front end mates with the trigger link pin.

With the hammer at rest, pulling the trigger draws the trigger bar forward. The trigger bar stirrup is lifted by the trigger spring so that its inner face engages the forward edge of the inverted V-shaped, double-action notch in the right sector of the hammer, below the pivot. This pulls the bottom of the hammer forward, rotating its top to the rear, pushing the hammer strut down, and compressing the hammer spring. As the hammer rotates, the cam on its center sector acts against the sear spur to rotate it forward, raising its forward arm against the firing-pin lock and lifting it to unlock the firing pin. When the hammer's arc of rotation approaches 35 degrees, the rear edge of the double-action cocking notch contacts the top of the trigger bar stirrup, pushing it down and disengaging it from the hammer, which then rotates forward under pressure from its spring. As the contact between the hammer and trigger bar breaks, continuing pressure of the shooter's finger on the trigger moves the single-action spur on the trigger bar into contact with the activating lug on the sear, holding it in position to maintain pressure from its forward arm on the firing-pin lock. The hammer spring acts through the hammer strut to drive the hammer forward until the rebound shoulder on its center sector contacts the front of the hammer strut; at this point the striking face of the hammer is approximately 3 mm from the rear of the firing pin. The strut disengages from the strut pin and is moved backward by the hammer's inertia working through the rebound shoulder, recompressing the hammer spring slightly. Inertia continues the hammer's forward rotation until it strikes the rear of the firing pin, driving it forward and firing the chambered cartridge; then the hammer spring, acting through the hammer strut on the hammer's rebound shoulder, moves the hammer back out of contact with the firing pin until the hammer spring pressure on the rebound shoulder and strut pin is equalized.

As the slide recoils, compressing the recoil spring, the front of the disconnector cut in its lower right side rides over the disconnector cam on the top of the trigger bar, pushing it downward and disengaging it from the sear. The sear spring rotates the sear back into its resting position, allowing its activating lug to ride over the top of the trigger bar spur and preventing it from reengaging the sear. The rear of the slide rotates the hammer to the rear, pressing the hammer strut down and compressing the hammer spring.

The slide's rearward movement is arrested by contact with the front face of the disassembly button and the firing pin's inertia moves it into its rear, locked position; the recoil spring then drives the slide forward, clearing the hammer, which rotates forward until the cocking step on its center sector stops against the sear spur, holding it in the cocked position. As the slide closes, its disconnector cut clears the top of the disconnector cam on the trigger bar, which remains out of engagement with its spur trapped under the activating lug of the sear. When the shooter relaxes finger pressure on the trigger its spring rotates it forward, moving the trigger bar to the rear. When the trigger bar spur clears the sear-activating lug, the trigger spring pushes it upward into engagement with the rear face of the lug, readying it for single-action firing. (When the hammer is cocked manually, the single-action setup notch in its right sector engages the rear of the trigger bar, pushing it downward and forward into the approximate position for single-action firing; when finger pressure is then applied to the trigger, the trigger spring lifts the rear of the trigger bar into contact with the activating lug on the sear, ready for firing.)

Pulling the trigger in the single-action mode moves the trigger bar forward, but since the hammer is cocked, the trigger bar stirrup passes under the double-action notch; the trigger bar spur contacts the activating lug on the sear and rotates it forward. The sear's rotation lifts its forward arm, pushing the firing-pin lock up and disengaging it from the firing pin, while simultaneously breaking contact between the sear spur and the cocking step on the hammer. The hammer rotates forward under pressure from its spring and the cycle continues as described above, firing the chambered cartridge and setting up the next single-action shot. When the hammer and trigger are at rest, the sear spur is positioned below the safety step on the hammer, preventing the hammer from contacting the rear of the firing pin if impacted.

Hold-Open Catch/Ejector

The hold-open catch is a bar that is 61 mm long, with a 90-degree bend at its front forming a lug that interacts with its spring, a pivot pin hole just to the rear of this bend, a spur or lug (depending on type) on its lower edge to the rear of its center, projecting to the right into the magazine well, and its top rear folded 90 degrees to the right to interact with the slide breech face; a 1 mm step on the right side of the angled section serves as the ejector. When the slide opens over a loaded magazine, the rear of the hold-open catch rides in a groove on

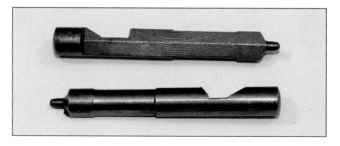

Firing pin, left and right sides

the bottom left of the breech face; if a cartridge is being extracted from the chamber its rim strikes the ejector, rotating the cartridge case to the right around the extractor claw and ejecting it through the port in the slide. The slide is then driven forward by the recoil spring, riding over the catch to chamber the next cartridge.

When the slide opens over an empty magazine, the left front of the magazine follower contacts the activating spur (or lug, depending on type) on the hold-open catch, rotating its rear upward into line with the breech face. When the slide reaches its rear limit of travel the recoil spring drives it forward until the breech face contacts the rear of the hold-open catch, arresting its forward movement. The pressure of the slide on the rear of the catch locks the parts together, holding the slide open while the magazine is being removed and replaced. When the empty magazine has been removed or a loaded magazine is in place, pulling the slide slightly to the rear releases the hold-open catch, which is rotated out of engagement with the breech face by its spring, allowing the slide to return to battery when released.

Extractor and Cartridge Indicator

The extractor is 30 mm long, with a claw at its front end, a relief cut in its top for the extractor spring, and a slot in its upper rear end that mates with the cartridge indicator. It is housed in a flat horizontal slot in the right side of the slide and rotates around a vertical pin centered 12 mm behind its front edge; it is activated by a coil spring with extended ends that pushes its rear to the right, rotating the claw to the left against the breech face. The cartridge indicator is a modified cylinder 5 mm in diameter and 20 mm long that rides in a transverse horizontal tunnel above the firing pin, centered 15 mm to the rear of the extractor pin; its left end is contoured to match the curvature of the slide, and the right three-quarters of its length is reduced to 4 mm in diameter, with its lower side relieved to ride over the firing pin and the extractor, leaving a 2 mm diameter lug protruding downward near its right end that rides in the groove at the rear of the extractor. When the extractor is at rest against an empty chamber the left end of the cartridge indicator is flush with the surface of the slide, but when a cartridge is chambered its rim rotates the front of the extractor to the right and its rear to the left, pushing the left end of the cartridge indicator 1 mm out of the side of the slide to provide both visible and tactile evidence that the chamber is loaded. The left shoulder of the relief cut in the bottom of the cartridge indicator is designed to intrude slightly into the firing-pin tunnel below it; this prevents the firing pin from being installed incorrectly.

Firing Pin and Firing-Pin Lock

The firing pin is a modified cylinder, 5 mm in diameter and 44 mm long with a 1.5 mm diameter tip 3.5 mm long at its front end. A 2.5 mm deep, double-beveled clearance cut for the firing-pin lock

Firing pin with firing-pin lock in locked position

Hold-open catch and spring

The cartridge indicator is located on the left side of the slide, above the gripping grooves, and protrudes when the chamber is loaded.

Extractor and cartridge indicator, showing linkage

begins on the right side of the pin 5 mm forward of its rear and extends all the way forward to the base of the tip; a locking notch in the pin's top also begins 5 mm from the rear and extends 10 mm forward, its rear half beveled to form a cam and its front half 2.5 mm deep. An additional circumferential relief zone 0.5 mm deep begins 10 mm forward of the locking notch and extends another 11 mm forward to reduce friction. The firing-pin lock is also cylindrical, 5 mm in diameter and 12 mm long, with a 3 mm diameter hole in its top to accommodate its spring. A 3 mm deep clearance cut for the firing pin on the lock's left side begins 6 mm below its top and extends to its bottom, with the lower 1.5 mm beveled to reduce its depth by 1 mm, matching the lower face on the firing-pin clearance cut and providing a larger contact area for interaction with the sear. The firing-pin lock spring is 2 mm in diameter and 9 mm long, with a coil enlarged at one end to grip the inside of its recess in the lock.

When the parts are at rest, the firing pin is in its rearward position with its tip withdrawn from the breech face, retained in that position by pressure from the firing-pin lock spring, which holds the lock against the bottom of the locking notch in the pin. In this position, the firing pin cannot reach the primer on a chambered cartridge. When the trigger is fully pulled, it acts through the trigger bar to rotate the sear, raising its front arm against the bottom of the firing-pin lock and lifting it. This unlocks the firing pin, leaving it in its rear position where the falling hammer strikes it, driving it forward through the breech face and firing the chambered cartridge. As the slide moves to the rear under recoil, the bottom of the firing-pin lock slides off the front sear arm, allowing its spring to move it downward against the cam surface in the firing-pin notch. When the slide reaches its rear limit of travel, the combination of the firing pin's rearward inertia and the pressure of the lock on its cam surface moves it into its rear position, allowing the lock to seat in the bottom of the locking notch. The firing pin then remains locked until the firing cycle is repeated.

Safety and Decocking Mechanism

The safety has a modified cylindrical body 9 mm in diameter and 15 mm long; a flange at its left end is enlarged to a diameter of 10 mm, with a lever at

Safety

Comparison of vz. 50-70 (*left*) and vz. 52 safeties, showing difference in depth of detent grooves. The deeper grooves of the vz. 50-70 safety are much more effective in preventing discharge during decocking.

its top extending tangentially forward 15 mm from the centerline of the cylinder, with a 3 mm grooved gripping sector projecting to the left at its forward end. A small locking lug projects 1.5 mm from the right end of the safety body and interacts with the trigger bar. A cut in the body that is 8 mm long encompasses the sear spur and is divided into two sectors, the right sector allowing the base of the hammer to rotate through it and the left sector containing a shoulder that interacts with the sear spur and the left sector of the hammer base during decocking. Two 1 mm deep detent grooves are cut into the opposite side of the safety body from the hammer / sear cut to engage the spring-loaded safety detent mounted in the receiver.

When the safety is in the "fire" position (with the lever up), a red-painted recess on the left side of the receiver is exposed, indicating readiness to fire, and the safety detent is seated in its rear groove, retarding movement of the safety. The cut sectors in the safety body are aligned to allow free movement of the hammer and sear and the safety locking lug is raised and does not block movement of the trigger bar. If the trigger is pulled, the firing mechanism will operate normally to fire the pistol.

When the safety is in the "safe" position (with the lever two-thirds of the way down), the red-painted recess in the receiver is covered, indicating that the pistol is not ready to fire and the safety detent is seated in its front groove, again retarding movement of the safety. The safety cutout does not prevent the hammer from moving, allowing it to be cocked, but the safety lug is lowered into the locking notch on the trigger bar, preventing it from contacting the sear. Attempting to pull the trigger will not fire the pistol.

When the hammer is cocked and the safety lever is pushed downward past the "safe" position, the shoulder of the left sector in the safety cutout pushes the sear spur forward, disengaging it from the hammer while simultaneously moving into the path of the safety shoulder on the hammer's left sector. The hammer rotates forward under pressure from its spring and as its bottom passes through the right sector of the safety cutout, the cam surface above the cocking notch on the hammer's center sector applies pressure to the safety, ensuring that the shoulder in the safety's left sector intercepts the safety shoulder on the hammer, stopping it before it reaches the rear of the firing pin to prevent the pistol from firing and leaving the hammer uncocked and at rest.

Unlike the decocking mechanism of the vz. 52 army pistol, in which the falling hammer cams the safety all the way back to the "safe" position before being stopped by the safety shoulder, the vz. 50-70 mechanism does not reset the safety but intercepts the hammer directly. The vz. 52 safety has a much-weaker detent mechanism and can, under some circumstances, allow the hammer to apply enough rotary inertia to force the safety to rotate past "safe" to the "fire" position during decocking, resulting in unintended firing. The vz. 50-70 safety detent is much more robust and is not subject to this type of accident. However, if the safety detent spring is shortened, weakened, or improperly replaced, or if the detent plunger is damaged or missing, unintended firing during decocking is possible. Any vz. 50-70 with a safety that does not latch firmly in the "fire" and "safe" positions should be unloaded and removed from service until the problem is corrected. Before use, vz. 50-70 pistols should be subjected to the "dowel" safety checks described in chapter 10 to ensure that the decocking mechanism is functioning properly.

Disassembly Button

Disassembly button with spring and screw, viewed from the front

The disassembly button has a body that is 10 mm wide and 12 mm long, with an inverted T-shaped cross section; its right end has a bottom extension projecting 10 mm down and 8 to 9 mm farther to the right, depending on type, with a checkered or grooved control surface. The left end of the body has a threaded vertical hole for its mounting screw and the inner face behind the control surface on the right has a 3 mm diameter hole to accept its operation spring, which is seated in a transverse hole in the receiver below the button's body. The lower center front of the body has a clearance slot 3 mm wide and 2 mm deep to allow entry of a lug in the inside bottom front of the slide during disassembly.

The button rides in a transverse slot in the receiver above the front of the trigger guard that matches its cross section. When it is at rest, its spring presses it to the right as far as its mounting screw allows, extending its control surface past the right side of the slide. During recoil, the front slide lug strikes the front of the disassembly button body to the right of its clearance cut, arresting the slide's rearward movement and preventing the rear slide grooves from disengaging from their rails on the receiver. When the button is pressed all the way to the left and the slide is drawn to the rear, the front slide lug enters the clearance notch on the disassembly button body, allowing the rear of the slide grooves to clear the receiver rails and be lifted off the receiver for disassembly. When the slide is being reinstalled, fully depressing the button again allows the front slide lug to enter the clearance notch, so the rear slide grooves can be lowered into alignment with the receiver rails and returned to battery.

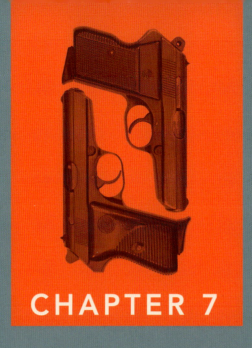

CHAPTER 7

Disassembly and Assembly

For those who are not mechanically inclined, disassembly of vz. 50-70s should be avoided unless necessary; a corollary of Murphy's law ("If anything can go wrong, it will go wrong, and at the worst possible time") is "Disassembly is always easier than reassembly, especially if springs and small parts are involved." In other words, "If it ain't broke, don't fix it." However, those who collect used pistols will usually encounter specimens that contain fouling or dried grease, have worn or broken parts, or for other reasons require maintenance or repair involving disassembly. The author routinely removes the firing pin and its lock from any newly acquired pistol of this type and cleans them and their recesses in the slide, because experience has demonstrated that these parts usually have grease, oil, or fouling that will eventually cause problems, and the task is relatively quick and simple. In many cases, removing the grip panels, soaking the receiver assembly in solvent, and swabbing or blowing out the residue is effective for removing oil and grease; compressed air is a wonderful cleaning agent. (Read and follow all label directions when using solvents; diesel fuel is not recommended for this use because it is not labeled for it and carries significant risk of chronic toxicity from dermal exposure.) Complete disassembly may not be necessary; if a broken trigger spring is the problem, you will need to dismount the hammer and remove the sideplate, but leave the sear and safety undisturbed and you won't have to worry about re-assembling them. If a tight magazine catch needs adjustment, don't disturb the firing mechanism. Some pistols are easy to work with, while others seem to have demons that interfere with everything, perhaps from small variances in machining of key parts. Vz. 50-70s are not unusually complex, but if you find disassembly challenging, it may be preferable to leave the job to a gunsmith.

In nearly three decades of working with vz. 50-70s and mechanically similar vz. 52s, the author has encountered most of the problems—and made most of the mistakes—that are likely to occur. (He once completed assembly of a vz. 50, noticed that the slide had an unusual rattle, and discovered that he had failed to install the recoil spring!) There were no comprehensive technical manuals or videos available on the subject in the early 1990s and repair or rebuilding these pistols was a process of trial and error. This chapter has been written with a view toward offering multiple methods of accomplishing difficult tasks, since someone attempting to repair a single pistol may not want to invest time and money in special tools that a gunsmith would find useful. Some special circumstances are discussed at the end of the chapter, and it is recommended that the entire chapter be read and understood before beginning disassembly.

Disassembly and Assembly

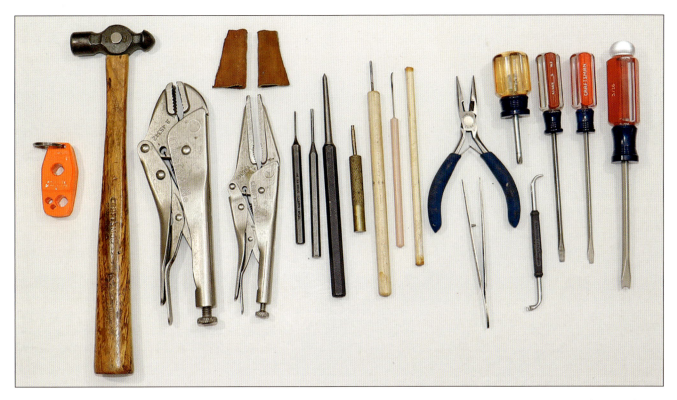

Author's tool kit for vz. 50-70 disassembly and assembly. Small, round object on hammer head is a supermagnet; brown objects above small locking-jaw pliers are leather sleeves; orange item to left is a tool magnetizer.

Tools

Some steps in the disassembly/reassembly process can be difficult and even dangerous without proper tools. Dismounting and reinstalling the hammer spring retainer is a particular problem and methods prescribed for it in some respected publications are, in the author's opinion, ill advised. Assembling the sear and its spring can also be challenging and protective eyewear should be worn when performing both of these tasks because of the risk of springs and associated parts flying off under tension. You will need a small hammer and a ³⁄₃₂" steel punch to remove and install most pins. A ¹⁄₁₆" punch is needed to remove the hold-open catch pin and a center or staking punch is used in reinstalling it. A longer tool of ¹⁄₁₆" or slightly larger diameter is needed to back the firing pin out for removal; a standard ¹⁄₁₆" pin punch is only 4" long, barely extending past the front of the slide when inserted into the firing-pin hole and thus difficult to manipulate, so the author uses a 6" length of ³⁄₈" dowel with the shaft of a 4d finishing nail mounted in one end, which is inexpensive, easy to make, and effective, and its mild steel tip will not damage the firing pin. A special tool facilitates maneuvering the sear into place during installation; options for constructing it are included below. A "teasing needle" like the ones included in high school dissecting kits, with its tip heated and bent to form a small hook, can be used to extract stuck or broken safety detent, disassembly button, and hold-open catch springs. A brass punch may be useful to loosen parts immobilized by dried oil or grease. A ⅛" flat-blade screwdriver is used to remove the grip screw (this screw is actually ³⁄₁₆", but the slot is too narrow for most American screwdrivers of that size). Another ⅛" screwdriver can be modified for use in magazine disassembly, as described below. While a ⅛" flat-blade screwdriver can be used to remove the take-down button screw if it is not tightly set, a low-profile 4 mm offset screwdriver may be needed to break it free; the author had difficulty finding such a tool and modified a standard 4 mm offset screwdriver to make it fit. A ¼" flat-blade screwdriver helps prevent the hammer pivot from turning during disassembly and assembly on post-1971 vz. 70s and a 7 mm box or crescent wrench is needed to remove the hammer pivot nut. A round, 4–4.5 mm diameter tool is needed to depress the firing-pin lock when removing and installing the firing pin; the author uses a #1 Phillips screwdriver with its tip ground flat for this purpose. A small pair of locking-jaw pliers with its jaws padded by leather sleeves is useful for depressing the disassembly button while removing its retaining screw,

Czech Cold War Police Pistols

Chapter 7

Assembly/disassembly cradle (the author's cradle also accommodates the vz. 52)

grasping the rear of the firing pin during removal and positioning the magazine spring tip during reassembly, and a pair of tweezers may be needed to remove the safety detent. A small supermagnet is useful for holding small parts in place during assembly, and a 6" length of ¼" dowel with its ends sealed with wood glue is used for the firing-pin function and safety tests described in chapter 10.

While a vise with padded jaws can be used to hold the pistol's receiver during dismounting and installation of the hammer spring retainer and sear, leaving both hands free, the author recommends the use of a simple wooden cradle for these tasks, avoiding the risk of damaging the receiver. The cradle consists of a section of 2" × 6" or larger wooden board approximately 12" long, with two parallel 1" × 2" wooden rails fastened to one side, aligned with the board's long axis and ⅞" (22 mm) apart. A transverse saw cut ¼" deep accommodates the pistol's rear sight, and a strip of Velcro attached to the cradle to secure the front of the pistol's receiver (just forward of the trigger guard) prevents it from tipping backward during hammer spring retainer removal and installation. Small wooden or plastic wedges or shims are used to secure the receiver in a partially upright position during sear installation.

and the same tool, with the outsides of the jaws ground down to improve clearance, can be used when installing the sear pin and as an alternative for gripping the hammer spring retainer during dismounting and reassembly. A better tool for dealing with the hammer spring retainer, especially for those who frequently disassemble vz. 50-70s, is a pair of ½" wide-jaw locking pliers modified as described below. A small pair of needlenose pliers is useful for

Vz. 70, field stripped

Field Stripping

Remove the magazine and clear the pistol to ensure that it is unloaded. Grip the pistol with the right hand in the firing position, push the disassembly button to the left with the right index finger (as far as it will go), draw the slide all the way to the rear with the left hand, lift its rear clear of the receiver, and allow the recoil spring to move it forward under control until it clears the barrel. (An alternative method is to hook the right index finger around the front of the trigger guard and, with the muzzle pointing to the right, depress the disassembly button with the right thumb and retract the slide with the left hand; in some cases, it may be necessary to use padded locking-jaw pliers to fully depress the disassembly button.) Separate the slide and recoil spring from the receiver. Use a ⅛" flat-blade screwdriver to remove the grip screw and separate the grip panels from the receiver.

Pistols are sometimes encountered with disassembly buttons that do not align properly with the slide lug, making removal of the slide difficult; it may be necessary to use a pair of padded locking-jaw pliers to depress the button far enough to release the slide. Remove the disassembly button as described below, withdraw its spring, and clean its recesses to remove any dried grease, foreign matter, or spring fragments that could impair its operation. Replace the spring if it is kinked or damaged and recheck the button for proper function; if it still fails to mate properly with the slide lug, use a jeweler's file to bevel the left edge of its recess in the button and the corresponding corner of the slide lug until they mate acceptably.

Another problem that can make slide removal difficult is a recoil spring with its front coil, which is larger in diameter than the rear, wound a little too far, creating a double coil that blocks the slide from moving far enough to the rear to clear the receiver; it will also pinch the barrel when the rear of the slide is lifted, making it difficult both to remove or reinstall it. This is difficult to diagnose because you can't see the cause of the problem, but if you can't get the slide to release even with the disassembly button clamped down, stand a piece of ⅜" inside-diameter pipe at least 3" long on your workbench, place the muzzle of the pistol against it (with the front of the barrel inside the pipe), and, holding the grip frame, press the muzzle into the pipe, forcing the slide to the rear until it can be removed from the receiver. Trimming off about one-quarter of the spring's front coil should resolve this issue.

Magazine

The magazine floor plate is retained by the projecting tip of the magazine spring, which engages a notch in the floor plate's left side. On magazines without finger rests, a ⅛" flat-blade screwdriver can be used to lift the spring tip into the slot in the bottom left of the magazine body, releasing the floor plate and

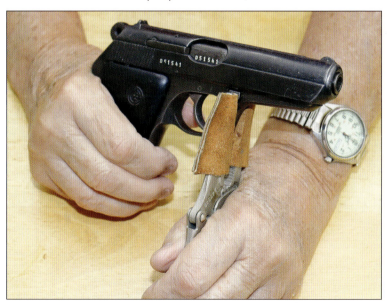

Using small, padded locking-jaw pliers to retract the disassembly button when slide removal is difficult (this technique is also used when removing the retaining screw to dismount the disassembly button).

A ⅛" flat-blade screwdriver modified to dismount magazine spring tip when removing finger-rest magazine floor plate

allowing it to be drifted forward off the magazine (be careful to restrain the magazine spring during floor plate removal, or it will be ejected forcefully when released). On magazines with finger rests, it is much more difficult to lift the spring tip into the slot and hold it there while the floor plate is being removed; a much-simpler method is to push the spring tip directly into the magazine body, using a modified ⅛" screwdriver with a small notch filed in one corner of its tip so the remaining blade completely fills the slot. Once the spring tip clears the slot, its tension will snap it to one side, allowing the floor plate to be removed without obstruction. Do not force the floor plate, since the finger rest is fragile and easily broken; if it does not move with moderate pressure, stop and determine the cause before proceeding. During reassembly, use a fingertip to depress the spring while starting the magazine base onto its rails on the bottom of the body, then use needlenose pliers to guide the spring tip into its slot. Bending the bottom coil of the spring outward slightly may help to make the tip engage properly.

Slide

The firing pin, its lock, and its lock spring can be removed by turning the slide upside down, using a 4 mm diameter tool to press the lock into the slide as far as it will go, and, while holding it in that position, inserting a punch or probe through the muzzle opening into the firing-pin hole in the breech face, pushing the firing pin back until its notch clears the lock and its rear protrudes at least ¼" from the rear of its recess; it may be necessary to tap the tool with a mallet to move the firing pin if it is heavily fouled or rusty. Use needlenose pliers to grasp the rear of the firing pin and remove it, then remove the firing-pin lock and spring from their recess. If the bottom of the slide is heavily peened at the rear of the lock recess as described and illustrated in chapter 10, it may be necessary to clamp the lower extension of the lock with a pair of narrow locking-jaw pliers and twist it several times to free it; the peened edges of the recess will then need to be dressed with a jeweler's file before reassembly. (*Warning*: DO NOT

Using a modified #1 Phillips screwdriver to compress the firing-pin lock spring while dismounting the firing pin with a probe

Disassembly and Assembly

attempt to install the slide on the receiver, even temporarily, with the firing pin removed and the lock still in place, since the lock, under spring pressure, will drop into the firing-mechanism recess in the receiver and lodge there, preventing the slide from being removed. Remedies for this problem are discussed at the end of this chapter.)

With the firing pin removed, use a ³⁄₃₂" punch to drift the extractor pin downward out of the slide, allowing the punch to follow the pin into its hole to prevent the extractor from springing free (extractor pins are occasionally encountered that are unusually tight, requiring a heavier hammer to drift them out). With the extractor restrained, withdraw the punch and remove the extractor and its spring to the right, disengaging the cartridge indicator, which can then be removed to the left. When reassembling these parts, the longer arm of the extractor spring must face the extractor and the extractor pin must pass through the spring's loop; it is easiest to assemble the parts by using a punch inserted from the bottom of the slide to temporarily retain them, then install the pin from the top, displacing the punch as it passes through the extractor. Before reassembling the slide, moisten a cotton swab with isopropyl alcohol, insert it in the rear of the firing-pin tunnel, and mop out any oil and carbon fouling; repeat with fresh, moist swabs until they come out clean and finish with a dry swab (the alcohol will dissolve oil and grease and absorb any water that is present). If there is rust or heavy fouling in the tunnel, a .22-caliber bore brush can be used to loosen it. The smaller firing-pin hole in the breech face is only 1.5 mm long and any fouling in it should be wicked out by the swab, but if there is concern, moisten the pointed end of a wooden toothpick with alcohol, insert it in the hole, and twist it to remove any residue (the author's improvised probe fits the firing-pin hole closely enough to remove any fouling that may be present). Repeat the cleaning process with the

Modified locking-jaw pliers for dismounting and installing the hammer spring retainer

Using a ⁵⁄₁₆" screwdriver blade to unseat the hammer spring retainer. Always use protective eyewear!

Gripping the hammer spring retainer for dismounting and installation with locking-jaw pliers

Czech Cold War Police Pistols

firing-pin lock and cartridge indicator recesses. Do not oil the firing pin, firing-pin lock, or cartridge indicator, since oil will collect dust and fouling and congeal over time, in some cases preventing the pistol from firing, and oil on the cartridge indicator will be transferred to the firing pin by capillary action; it is best to keep these parts clean and dry. Do not remove the rear sight unless replacement is necessary; it can be drifted to either side for removal, but when the replacement is installed, trial-and-error lateral adjustment will be necessary for proper alignment. Stake the sight in place after correct alignment has been achieved.

Firing Mechanism

The first step in disassembling the firing mechanism is removal of the hammer spring retainer; the Czechs probably had a special tool for this task, but the author had to develop his own methods to accomplish it. Place the receiver, with the slide temporarily installed, upside down in the cradle with the hammer at rest; use protective eyewear and keep your face clear of the work area. The hammer spring retainer must be pressed downward against its spring until it clears its notch in the grip frame; it then can be moved slightly to the rear and allowed, under control, to rise clear of its spring and be lifted off its strut, which can then be removed with the hammer spring and magazine retainer spring (if present). The author first accomplished this by using the tip of a ⅜" flat-blade screwdriver to depress the hammer spring retainer, but this provides little control of the parts when released, sometimes allowing them to fly off under spring tension. The second method used was to clamp a small pair of locking-jaw pliers onto one side of the hammer spring retainer and depress it using both hands, but the imbalance of force again made controlling the parts difficult. The author then purchased a larger pair of locking-jaw pliers described above, used a Dremel rotary tool to cut a slot 2 mm wide and 5 mm deep in the center of the upper jaw to accommodate the hammer strut, and made a semicircular cut 8 mm in diameter in the center of the lower jaw to accommodate the hammer spring. This allows the tool to straddle the hammer spring and strut and be locked securely onto the hammer spring retainer, controlling it safely with both hands during removal and reinstallation. (If you leave the tool clamped onto the hammer spring retainer after dismounting it, you won't have to realign it for reinstallation.)

With the hammer strut and spring removed, expose the firing mechanism by using a 7 mm box or crescent wrench to remove the hammer pivot nut; if the hammer pivot is the revised type, a screwdriver may be needed to prevent its head from turning during this process. On pistols with key-type hammer pivot heads (all vz. 50s and vz. 70s below about serial number J15000), the trigger bar rides in a notch near the right end of the pivot and must be pressed downward to clear this notch before the pivot can be removed; on later pistols with slotted pivot heads the shoulder near the right end has been set back, eliminating the notch, so this is not necessary. Withdraw the pivot and lift the hammer from the top of the receiver. Turn the pistol with its right side up and use a hammer and ³⁄₃₂" punch to drift the trigger and sear pins approximately 4 mm to the left, clear of the sideplate. Pull the sideplate slightly to the rear (a hammer and brass punch may be used against the inside of the hammer pivot hole if the sideplate does not move freely). Lift the rear of the sideplate, free its front flange from the receiver, and remove it. Lift the magazine catch and its spring out of their receiver recess. Note the positions of the hooked and straight ends of the sear spring and use a ³⁄₃₂" punch to drift the sear pin to the left out of the receiver, capturing the sear spring on the punch to prevent it from flying free; remove the sear from the receiver and then remove the punch, separating the sear from its spring. Lift the rear of the trigger bar, unhook it from the end of the trigger spring, and lift its front

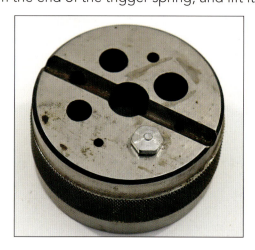

Bench block with mandrel, made from a ¼" machine screw to support the head of the hold-open catch pin while spreading the opposite end

off the trigger link pin. Lift the trigger with its spring and link pin out of the receiver and separate them, then drift the trigger pin out of the left side of the receiver. Turn the safety lever counterclockwise past the "safe" detent position to three o'clock; this will allow the safety detent to move out of its receiver recess under the shoulder of the safety. Use tweezers to extract the detent and its spring from their receiver recess and pull the safety to the left out of the receiver. If the safety detent spring does not come out with the detent, turn the receiver upside down after the safety has been removed and tap it against a wooden block or other nonmarring surface until inertia draws the spring out. If this doesn't work, use the modified "teasing needle" described above to snag the spring and draw it out. A fouled or rusted spring will not improve with age, so it should be removed and cleaned or replaced. If there is rust or dried grease in the detent spring recess a 3/32" drill bit may be used to manually ream it out, but do not use it with a power tool, since accidentally deepening the recess can prevent the detent from functioning properly. A pipe cleaner can be used to ensure that the recess is clean.

Hold-Open Catch

Do not remove the hold-open catch unless it is necessary for repair or replacement. If necessary, insert a 1/16" punch into the recess in the right end of the hold-open catch hinge pin and use a hammer to drift the pin to the left out of the receiver, taking care not to damage the edges of the recess at the right end of the pin. Restrain the catch while removing the punch, then lift the catch and its spring from the receiver. When reassembling the catch, the right end of the pin must be spread after installation with a center or staking punch to retain it; it should be tight enough to prevent lateral movement of the catch while allowing it to move vertically with enough freedom to function correctly. A mandrel fashioned to support the head of the pin while it is being spread simplifies this task.

Disassembly Button

To remove the disassembly button, first use a padded vise or padded locking-jaw pliers to fully depress and hold it. Do not overtighten the clamping device, since this will bind the screw and make removal more

Modified 4 mm offset screwdriver used to loosen and tighten the disassembly button screw

difficult; use only enough force to hold the button down. Use a compact or modified 4 mm offset screwdriver to loosen the disassembly button-retaining screw; once it is started, a smaller jeweler's screwdriver may be used to "tease" it out of the top left of the button. Release the clamping device and the button and its spring may be withdrawn to the right. Check the spring and its recess for damage, dried grease, or foreign matter before reassembly.

Barrel

Barrel removal requires a barrel press with a tail block machined to fit the rear of the vz. 50-70 chamber face. This tooling is not readily available and will usually have to be made to order by a machinist, which is relatively expensive. Removal of the barrel pin is required before pressing the barrel out of the receiver. When installing the replacement barrel, the

Barrel press

Chapter 7

extractor cut must be aligned with the matching receiver cut; if a new barrel is used, the barrel pin hole will need to be redrilled through the lower edge of the barrel and an extractor cut may have to be machined to match the one in the receiver. This type of work is best performed by a qualified gunsmith who is familiar with the vz. 50-70.

Firing-Mechanism Assembly

Before reassembling the pistol, it is helpful to identify the pins by length; the trigger hinge pin is 17 mm, the sear pin is 13 mm, and both the trigger pivot pin and extractor pin are 10 mm. (Mistakenly installing the trigger pin in place of the sear pin will bind the slide when it is being installed and the recoil spring, combined with the bind, will make it difficult to remove the slide and correct the problem.) The hold-open catch pivot pin has a head on the left end to retain it, while the right end is hollow and, as noted above, must be properly spread after installation to retain it. The hammer has a small transverse strut-bearing pin to the rear of its pivot hole that is staked in place and is not normally removed for cleaning and maintenance; if replacement is necessary, it should be restaked to secure it and its ends smoothed flush with the sides of the hammer. All parts should be clean and free of heavy oil or grease; a film of light oil or a small amount of dry powdered-graphite lubricant may be applied to bearing surfaces (except for the firing pin and associated parts) if desired.

Table 7-1 Parts Nomenclature	
1. Receiver with barrel	24. Hold-open catch
2. Slide	25. Hold-open catch pin
3. Rear sight	26. Hold-open catch spring
4. Firing pin	27. Disassembly button
5. Firing-pin lock	28. Disassembly button screw
6. Firing-pin lock spring	29. Disassembly button spring
7. Cartridge indicator	30. Safety
8. Recoil spring	31. Safety detent
9. Extractor	32. Safety detent spring
10. Extractor spring	33. Magazine catch
11. Extractor pin	34. Magazine catch spring
12. Sideplate	35. Sear
13. Trigger	36. Sear spring
14. Trigger bar	37. Sear pin
15. Trigger spring	38. Grip panel, right
16. Trigger pivot pin	39. Grip panel, left
17. Trigger link pin	40. Grip screw
18. Hammer pivot	41. Magazine body
19. Hammer pivot nut	42. Magazine follower
20. Hammer	43. Magazine spring
21. Hammer strut	44. Magazine floor plate, plain
22. Hammer spring	45. Magazine floor plate, rest
23. Hammer spring retainer	

Disassembly and Assembly

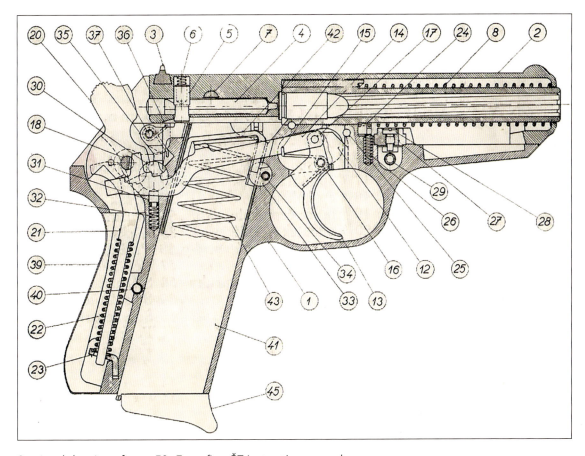

Sectional drawing of a vz. 50. *From first ČZ instruction manual*

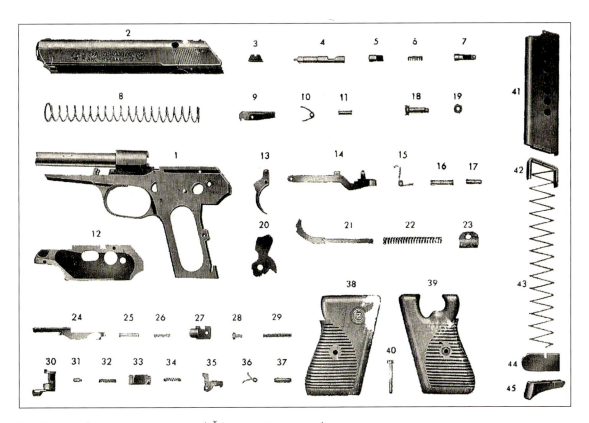

Vz. 50 parts diagrams. *From second ČZ instruction manual*

Czech Cold War Police Pistols   103

Installing the sear is tricky because you must push the sear assembly forward against spring pressure while either sliding the sear pin into a hole that is hidden by the sear itself or, with the sear and its spring assembled onto a slave pin, sliding the hole in the left side of the sear onto the end of the sear pin—also hidden—as it protrudes slightly into the firing mechanism recess in the receiver. Hold the safety with its lever pointing straight up and insert its body into its recess in the receiver, working it over and around the detent until it is properly seated. Press the lever forward until the interior shoulder contacts the detent and use the flat tip of a small screwdriver to depress the detent until the safety can be rotated to ride over it and latches in the "fire" position. Do not rotate the safety again until the rest of the firing mechanism and sideplate have been installed.

Installing the sear is tricky because you must push the sear assembly forward against spring pressure while either sliding the sear pin into a hole that is hidden by the sear itself or hooking the left side of the sear pin hole over the end of the pin—also hidden—protruding slightly into the firing-mechanism recess in the receiver. It is helpful to first slightly bevel the ends of the sear pin by chucking it into a drill and grinding it at a 45-degree angle against a whetstone; the objective is only to eliminate the sharp edge at the end of the pin and the resulting bevel should be barely visible.

Place the receiver in the cradle in a semiupright position, with the barrel angled downward and the grip frame secured by wooden or plastic wedges. For the "slave pin" method, insert the sear pin into its hole in the left side of the receiver until about 1 mm of it extends into the receiver recess. Insert the sear spring into its slot in the sear so that its coil is aligned with the pin hole, its long end points forward and down, and its shorter hooked end points to the right, across the top of the sear's forward arm. Apply a little petroleum jelly to the hammer pivot pin (which becomes the "slave" pin) to make it sticky and insert it into the pin hole in the sear so it passes through the coil of the spring, holding it in place. Use your right hand to guide the sear into position while your left hand presses the sear forward, compressing the spring, until the pin hole in the left side of the sear can be fitted onto the protruding end of the sear pin. Drift the sear pin to the right into the sear, capturing the spring and displacing the slave pin, leaving the end of the sear pin flush with the right side of the sear.

The problem with this method is that the receiver space for the sear is cramped and the fingers of the left hand, which are pressing the sear forward against spring pressure, block the view of the pin to which you are attempting to attach the sear. To facilitate the process, the author filed a semicircular notch in one end of a wooden ice cream stick, sanded one side until it was thin enough to fit into the spring slot in the sear, and used it to press the sear forward into position. Two halves of another ice cream stick were glued to the unnotched end, which was wrapped with friction tape for a better gripping surface, and the first sear tool was born (the Czechs probably had a better tool or jig for sear installation, but this was at least progress).

A second, more direct method of installation is to dispense with the slave pin, clamp one end of

Modified locking-jaw pliers with sear spring and pin correctly assembled for "direct" installation

"Direct" installation of the sear

104   The ČZ Models 50 and 70

the sear pin into the jaws of a pair of small locking-jaw pliers (which have been modified by trimming the outside surface of the jaws for clearance, as noted above), apply petroleum jelly to the pin, assemble the sear and its spring onto it, and press the pin into its hole in the receiver from the right, guiding it with the improvised sear tool. When the sear is in place, release the pliers and drift the sear pin to the left until its end is flush with the right side of the sear. This method can be more difficult than it sounds because it is hard to "find" the sear hole with the end of the pin, but with practice it is fairly simple.

The author eventually replaced his original sear tool with a sturdier version made by grinding a semicircular notch in the end of a ³⁄₁₆" flat-blade screwdriver, which offered a better view of the work area and a more comfortable handle, but each time he installed a sear, the question "Isn't there a better way to do this?" arose. The answer was to separate the spring installation from the sear installation, so you aren't fighting the spring while trying to align pins and holes in a place you can't see. The first attempts at this were disappointing; installing the sear with its pin inserted from the left just far enough to hold it while leaving the spring slot clear was simple, but getting the spring into position in its slot was not. The spring could be pre-positioned with a pair of tweezers, but when an effort was made to press it forward so the sear pin could be drifted through it, the spring leaped clear to fly away and hide in the most cluttered corner in the room (Murphy's law, again). Many hours were spent devising tools that could hold the spring while simultaneously pressing it into position and several workable solutions were developed, but they all violated the KISS principle: "Keep It Simple, Stupid." There was no point in developing a method that couldn't be easily replicated by other shooters and collectors. The solution was to magnetize the modified screwdriver, using a small key chain magnetizer/demagnetizer. The magnetizing is temporary but can be refreshed each time the tool is needed. Again, initial efforts with this technique ran into problems because the spring was difficult to balance on the narrow screwdriver tip and would snap back against the shaft, but at least it didn't fly away. The author ground the tip back to the point where it was just narrow enough to enter the spring slot in the sear, recut the notch, remagnetized the blade, and it held the spring effectively. Some care is still needed to retain the spring in the notch but it is fairly easy to insert the spring with the tool in the left hand, drift the sear pin through the sear with the right hand to capture the spring, and sear installation is complete. (If you have difficulty using both hands this way, have an assistant seat the pin after you position the spring.)

Insert the trigger pin in its hole in the left side of the receiver and drift it to the right until about 6 mm of its length is inside the trigger recess. Position the trigger spring in the trigger so its short end points toward the pistol's rear, its hooked end points upward and to the right, and the center of its coil is aligned with the trigger pivot pin hole. Insert the trigger link pin in the pivot pin hole to temporarily retain the spring in position, then press the trigger onto its pivot pin until the spring is captured by the pivot pin, displacing the link pin. Rotate the hooked end of the trigger spring counterclockwise until it passes the link pin hole and insert the link pin so it is forward of the hooked end of the trigger spring; the short end of the trigger spring should be seated against the bottom of its slot in the trigger. (It is possible to install the trigger spring with its short end resting against the front of the pivot pin and its hooked end pointing to the rear; the author has made this mistake and has observed it in newly purchased pistols that had evidently been assembled incorrectly. The result will be pinching of the hooked end of the spring between the rear of the trigger

Sear spring attached to modified and magnetized ³⁄₁₆" screwdriver for separate installation

Chapter 7

body and the bottom of the trigger bar, preventing the mechanism from functioning properly.)

Slip the front of the trigger bar under the hooked end of the trigger spring and fit its mounting hole onto the right end of the trigger link pin. Rotate the rear of the trigger bar into position in the hammer recess below the sear and safety. Install the magazine catch into its recess in the upper front of the magazine well and insert its spring into the hole in the right end of the catch. Slide the flange at the front of the sideplate into its slot in the right side of the receiver at the front of the trigger recess, press the sideplate's rear against the receiver, being careful not to crimp the magazine catch spring, and slide it forward until its rear is flush with the rear of the receiver; tapping its rear with a nonmarring mallet or wooden block may be necessary if the fit is tight. Drift the trigger and sear pins to the right, flush with the outside of the sideplate, securing it; check both ends of the sear pin to make sure they do not intrude into the slide grooves in the receiver and sideplate. With the safety in the "fire" position, work the trigger to make sure the trigger bar and sear move freely. Check the fit of the hammer pivot and its nut to make sure they mate properly; if the threads of either part have been staked, it may be necessary to make adjustments with a jeweler's file so they will work smoothly. Insert the hammer into the receiver from the top, reinstall the hammer pivot, working the trigger if necessary for clearance, and snug its nut against the sideplate; do not over-tighten it. Position the nut so that one of its flats faces the slide, so it won't interfere with slide travel. Using the left thumb to activate the hammer, pull the trigger to ensure that the firing mechanism is working smoothly. Apply a small drop of red Locktite to the threads at the right end of the hammer pivot to prevent it from working loose.

Hammer Spring and Associated Parts Assembly

Secure the receiver with slide installed upside down in the cradle, with the hammer uncocked; insert the hammer strut into the bottom of the hammer, with its curved end pointing to the rear; and slide the hammer spring onto the hammer strut. If the pistol is equipped with a magazine-retaining spring, it must be positioned in its grip frame recess so the hammer spring retainer will capture it when it is installed; a 9 mm diameter supermagnet can be placed on the inside of the magazine well to temporarily secure it during the process. Clamp the locking-jaw pliers securely onto the hammer spring retainer with its receiver flange pointing up, making sure that the tool does not block the hammer strut hole. Keeping your face clear of the work area, position the hammer spring retainer on the end of the hammer spring with its flange against the rear of the grip frame, press the retainer down onto the hammer strut and spring until the flange enters its receiver recess, and allow the hammer spring to seat the flange in the receiver recess. (If you are using a screwdriver blade or other tool rather than locking-jaw pliers, care will be needed to retain control of the hammer spring retainer during this process.) Remove the receiver from the cradle or vise and if the hammer spring retainer is not seated flush with the sides of the receiver, tap its side with a hammer to align it. Check the firing mechanism for proper function. Remove the slide, install the recoil spring, and re-install the slide.

Using a small supermagnet to hold the magazine-retaining spring in position while installing the hammer spring retainer

Special Circumstances

Pistols are occasionally encountered with the hammer locked in the cocked position, which prevents disassembly in the normal manner. If this happens, first remove the slide and try loosening the hammer pivot nut, which may unbind the hammer and allow it to be lowered and disassembly to proceed in the normal manner. (If the slide cannot be removed, have an assistant pull it to the rear until the disconnector cut is positioned above the hammer pivot nut and slowly unscrew it.) If this does not release the firing mechanism, place the receiver on its left side, remove the hammer pivot nut, push the trigger bar downward to clear the pivot, and use a hammer and a punch to drive the pivot to the left out of the receiver, capturing the hammer with the punch. Restrain the hammer with one hand and use the other to withdraw the punch, allowing the hammer and its strut, spring, and spring retainer to be removed from the top and rear of the receiver. Examine the hammer, sear, sear spring, safety, and trigger bar for damage and make sure there is no foreign matter present; it may be necessary to replace defective parts before reassembly.

In cases where the slide has been installed on the receiver with the firing pin removed and the firing-pin lock still in its recess, resulting in an internally locked slide, there are several possible remedies depending on the position of the lock. By itself, the lock spring will push the lock downward only about 2 mm below the edge of its recess, but in this situation, gravity is not your friend and can pull the lock farther into the firing mechanism. When you recognize that you have this problem, turn the pistol upside down and assess the situation. If the slide is stopped approximately 1 inch out of battery, the lock is lodged behind the sear; pull the slide slightly to the rear to release tension on the lock and strike the top of the slide smartly against a wooden block. This may retract the lock enough to allow the slide to be removed; if not, try the ice pick treatment described below. If this doesn't work, use the decocking function of the safety to partially lower the hammer, then remove the grip panels, dismount the hammer spring retainer, and remove the hammer spring, strut, and hammer pivot. This may allow the hammer to shift enough to permit the slide to be removed, but if not, you will have to go to forceful disassembly, below, which may damage the slide.

Initial position of firing-pin lock in its slide recess without the firing pin

Firing-pin lock captured and retracted with an ice pick

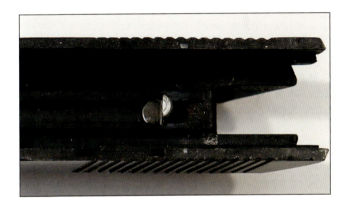

Position of firing-pin lock in its recess without the firing pin after repeated efforts to retract the slide

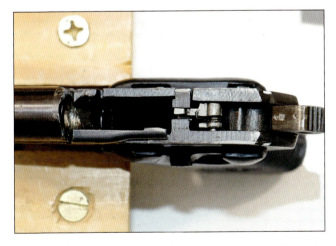

Top view of firing mechanism with hammer cocked. The firing-pin lock is normally positioned above the lug on the forward arm of the sear, with the slide in battery. If the firing pin is missing, the lock usually rests on top of the forward arm between the receiver bridge and the sear body, preventing the slide from moving more than a few millimeters in either direction. It can also lodge behind the sear body in the hammer space.

If the slide is stopped approximately ¼" out of battery, the lock is lodged against the receiver bridge that forms the rear of the magazine well, resting on the forward arm of the sear and prevented from moving more than a few millimeters to the rear by the sear body. Keeping the pistol upside down, shine a bright light into the firing-pin tunnel and see if the edge of the firing-pin relief cut in the bottom of the lock is visible in the top or upper right quadrant of your field of view. If it is visible, insert the tip of an ice pick into the opening and wriggle, push, or tap the shaft of the ice pick into the opening, forcing the lock deeper into its slide recess. Once you have forced the lock to retract at least 2.5 mm, leave the ice pick in place and turn the pistol upright, and you should be able to dismount the slide in the normal manner.

If no opening is visible and you can see only the body of the lock in the firing-pin tunnel, you can try relieving the slide pressure on the lock and striking the top rear of the slide against a wooden block, but this probably won't work; if you or someone else has tried repeatedly to move the slide back and forth in an effort to free it, the lock has probably been rotated 90 degrees by impacting the receiver bridge, leaving the outside of the lock's downward extension facing you. At this point your only option is forceful disassembly; remove the grip panels so they won't be damaged in the process.

You will need a ½" washer, a piece of ½"–⅜" inside-diameter steel pipe 4"–6" long, and a 16-to-20-ounce hammer. Clamp padded locking-jaw pliers over the disassembly button to hold it in the dismounting position. You are going to drive the slide backward off the receiver, bending or shearing off the firing-pin lock extension in the process, one hopes without damaging the slide or receiver; all other parts are replaceable. Set the rear of the pistol's grip frame on a solid wooden block or the edge of a strong wooden workbench, with the muzzle pointing up and the rear of the slide clear of obstruction. Place the washer around the barrel so it rests against and protects the front of the slide, fit the pipe onto the barrel (with one end resting on the washer), and push the slide to the rear as far as it will go to eliminate the cushioning effect of the recoil spring. Strike the upper end of the pipe with the hammer until the slide is driven far enough to the rear to disengage it from the receiver, then remove it in the normal manner along with the washer, pipe, and recoil spring. With the slide removed, extract the firing-pin lock; you may need to drill and tap a hole in it and install a screw to use as a handle to pull it out. After the lock is removed, clean the firing-pin and lock recesses in the slide to remove any residual metal fragments. Inspect the slide, sear, sear spring, hammer, and hammer pivot for damage and replace as necessary; make sure there are no residual fragments of the firing-pin lock in the receiver, and reassemble the pistol. (If the firing-pin lock recess in the slide has been distorted, it may be necessary to weld and redrill it; this should be done by an experienced gunsmith.)

Pistols are occasionally encountered that simply don't "want" to work properly; if this happens, stop, isolate the problem to the specific part or parts involved, and study the situation to understand what needs to be done to correct it. An example is 65-dated vz. 50 serial number B69414, which, on the basis of tool marks and other factors, was assembled from a slide and possibly a receiver fabricated before the 1963 production suspension and may have had some of the defects that forced operations to be reorganized, although that is speculative. Purchased as a "gunsmith special," this pistol had been refinished, probably by the Czech police department that owned it, and reassembled with an incorrect sideplate numbered 9717 which did not fit well, causing the slide to drag. It had evidently been through several repair attempts; its sear spur was broken (probably from being dropped on its hammer), its trigger bar had unusual wear suggesting binding, its trigger spring was improperly assembled, and it had an improvised extractor spring that was too weak to function. Despite a good deal of holster wear it showed little evidence of actual firing, suggesting that it might never have worked properly. After hand-fitting a replacement sideplate to match the receiver contours and slide mechanical surfaces, replacing the sear and extractor spring, and reassembling the mechanism properly, the hammer and sear displayed internal binding that prevented them from functioning reliably. The hammer bind occurred as it neared full cock, indicating a clearance issue with its bearing surfaces that did not prevent the mechanism from functioning but could retard hammer speed enough to prevent primer ignition. Since receiver bearing surfaces can be difficult to smooth without distortion, a hard Arkansas stone was used to dress both sides of the hammer bottom until it moved freely. The sear had visible free play between its left side and the interior of its receiver recess but would not move far enough to the left to contact the inside of the receiver, so the bind had to be on the right side, where its activating lug brackets the trigger bar and internal receiver flange supporting the safety. When the sear and sideplate were installed without the other firing-mechanism parts the sear rotated and moved laterally without difficulty, so the bind had to be caused by the trigger bar, which showed bright spots on both sides in the area that slides through the sear-operating lug. A flat file was used to dress both sides of the trigger bar in that area, smoothing it to remove high spots and thinning it slightly; this eliminated the bind and the pistol functioned as intended when reassembled.

Parts Compatibility

One of the persistent myths about the vz. 50-70 claims that the two models are completely different and parts are not interchangeable. This is not reflected in the pistols' manuals or ČZ company literature, but to test it the author took a stripped receiver from NB 50 serial number 669633 and a parts set from decommissioned 81-dated vz. 70 serial number △701523 and combined them. Some hand-fitting of the sideplate and slide was necessary, but everything else went together and functioned perfectly except for the hammer pivot pin, which had to be notched to fit the receiver recess key, and the hold-open catch, which was the late type introduced in 1976 and thus would not fit the smaller 1950 receiver recess. The author could have enlarged the recess with a jeweler's file to accept the late catch but chose to substitute an early catch instead. The resulting "hybrid" has become the author's shooter for most trips to the range and has digested more than five hundred rounds of FMJ ammunition without any malfunctions. The only parts incompatibilities are the hammer pivot pin and hold-open catch, as noted, and the inability of the early receiver to accommodate a magazine retaining spring. An original type takedown catch was installed as a matter of personal preference.

"Hybrid" pistol consisting of a vz. 70 slide, sideplate, and parts assembled on an early vz. 50 receiver

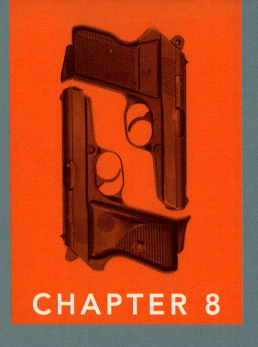

CHAPTER 8

Holsters and Accessories

Early holsters for the vz. 50 were adaptations of designs produced for the ČZ Model 27 during and immediately after World War II (this pistol is commonly called the ČZ 27 in the US but is referred to as the vz. 27 in this chapter). The holsters' similarity often leads to misidentification, so it is necessary to discuss those designed for the vz. 27 in order to define and describe their distinguishing characteristics. All vz. 50-70 holsters will accommodate the vz. 27, but due to the vz. 50-70's longer grip tang, flaps on vz. 27 holsters will not close on vz. 50-70s without considerable stretching and possible damage.

Vz. 27s saw widespread wartime use by German troops; early German occupation holsters were made of 6-ounce top-grain, split-cowhide leather, dyed either brown or black, and carry the encircled ČZ logo, **WaA76** inspection marks, German **P.Mod.27** identification, and 1940 to 1942 dates stamped on the rear below the flap fold. Holsters were made by a number of other manufacturers identified by German military letter codes; after 1942, 4-ounce leather was commonly used in smooth brown and black or black pebble-grain finishes, and after 1944 most holsters were undated and sometimes completely unmarked. Early postwar Czech vz. 27 holsters are dimensionally similar to wartime production but are made of 4-ounce tan or brown pebble-grain leather and are usually ink-stamped on the inside of the flap with the Czech lion and the maker's name, Adalbert Riedl. (A composite leather and green fabric holster was also made for the vz. 27 during this period, but it proved unsatisfactory and was discontinued.) After the 1948 Communist coup, privately owned companies were nationalized and there were a series of vicious political purges; many formerly prominent families were targeted and the Riedl family, among others, disappeared from public life. Holster markings were eliminated and the practice of embossing the leather or buffing its outer surface to produce a smooth finish was suspended. Manufacture of the vz. 27 continued until 1950, but the vz. 50 police pistol was already in development and the standard holster was expanded slightly to a transitional model that could accommodate both pistols. Holster closure straps were shortened and widened to reduce tearing around the stud hole, and probably to accommodate this change, the patterns used for cutting holster parts from hides were also changed, shortening the length of the magazine pouch. The differences between Communist-era vz. 27 holsters and transitional vz. 50 holsters are so minor that they were only recently recognized as separate types; the author's classification system for vz. 50-70 holsters was published in 2009, but since these holsters do not fit the system, the transitional label was used rather than creating confusion by revising the system. This classification system was developed for purposes of discussion only; labels used, with exception of the vz. 62 holster, are not based on Czech nomenclature.

The standard wartime vz. 27 holster has a body made from a single piece of leather with a closure flap that is 135 mm wide at its fold, and the closed holster is 185 mm long top to toe; open holsters are 265 mm long excluding the closure strap. The closure strap is riveted to the flap and fastens to a body-mounted stud that is usually padded on the inside; it is 43 mm long from stud hole to tip and 20 to 22 mm wide at the stud hole, sometimes tapering to 25 mm near the rounded tip. The magazine pouch is sewn to the front of the holster and is 100 mm long, with its opening perpendicular to its body and its lower edge 30 mm above the holster toe; it accepts the full length of a magazine. A single 50 mm wide belt loop is sewn to the holster's rear. (Measurements will vary slightly among holsters due to environmental conditions and wear.) Stitching utilizes white thread and edge welting may be present or absent. A vz. 27 pistol fits the holster snugly, allowing it to close without stretching, while a vz. 50 will enter the holster but the flap will not close over it without significant stretching or damage. Early postwar vz. 27 holsters, as noted above, are similar to wartime holsters except for materials and marking.

Wartime vz. 27 holster made from full-grain leather, closed and open to show magazine pouch. This specimen is undated and marked WaA721; it is thought to have been produced by Továrna na kožené výrobky Franěk in Dolní Beřkovice, Bohemia, which became Kozak Leather Co. Factory 6 after being nationalized following the 1948 Communist coup.

Chapter 8

Early postwar vz. 27 holster

Communist-era vz. 27 holster, closed; note the distance from magazine pouch bottom to holster toe compared to the wartime holster above.

Communist-era vz. 27 holster, open; note shorter magazine pouch with slanted opening.

Communist-era vz. 27 holsters are made from 6-ounce natural, full-grain (unfinished), split-cowhide leather; edge welting is applied to the body, flap, closure strap, magazine pouch, and belt loop. The body and flap may be made from a single piece of leather or from two pieces, double-stitched together just above the belt loop; closure studs are not padded. Stitching utilizes white thread. Dimensions are similar to wartime holsters except that the flap is 3–5 mm narrower, the closure strap is 28–30 mm wide, and the magazine pouch is 90 mm long with its opening slanting downward from front to rear; its lower edge is 46 mm above the holster toe. The shorter pouch with slanted top and the greater distance from the pouch bottom to holster toe are identifying features.

Transitional vz. 50 holsters are easily mistaken for Communist-era vz. 27 holsters unless they are measured or compared side by side. They are made from the same type of leather with similar edge welting and the body and flap may be made from a single piece of leather or from two pieces as described above. The closed flap is 140 mm wide at its fold and the closed holster is 190 mm long top to toe; open holsters are 280 mm long, excluding the closure strap. The closure strap may be 25 to

Holsters and Accessories

43 mm long from stud hole to tip and is 30 mm wide; the magazine pouch is 90 mm long, with its opening tapered downward front to rear and its lower edge 48 mm above the holster toe. Stitching utilizes white thread. A vz. 27 pistol fits the holster easily and a vz. 50 fits it snugly, allowing the flap to close with little or no stretching; used holsters often show an imprint from the vz. 50's grip tang on the inside of the flap. Overall length and the size, shape, and location of the magazine pouch are primary identifying features. Skramoušský and Badalík (1996, 254) do not describe this holster specifically but apply the term *rozšířený typ pouzdra* ("expanded-type holster") to those made for the vz. 50-70.

Posttransition holsters for the vz. 50 (except for the type 2) are made of 4-ounce buffed, natural, split-cowhide leather and are almost always unmarked and undated except for the type 5; the change from full-grain to buffed leather apparently occurred in 1952 during the transition from production of the vz. 50 to the vz. 52 army pistol at Strakonice, since all observed vz. 52 cowhide holsters are made of buffed leather. Stitching utilizes white thread except in the type 5. The **type 1** is dimensionally almost identical to the transitional holster except for the magazine pouch; bodies on all observed specimens are made from a single piece of leather. There is no edge welting; the closure flap is 141 mm wide at the fold and the holster's closed length top to toe is 190 mm. The closure strap is riveted to the flap and fastens to a padded stud on the body; it is 24 mm long from stud hole to tip and 30 mm wide. The magazine pouch is 98 mm long, and its opening tapers downward slightly from rear to front. A single 50 mm wide belt loop is sewn to the

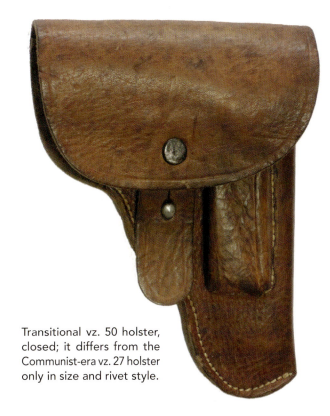

Transitional vz. 50 holster, closed; it differs from the Communist-era vz. 27 holster only in size and rivet style.

Communist-era vz. 27 holster (*left*) and transitional vz. 50 holster, showing comparative size; a magazine is inserted into vz. 27 pouch to show relative length. Note the magazine pouch's angled opening and the distance from its bottom to the holster toe.

Czech Cold War Police Pistols

Chapter 8

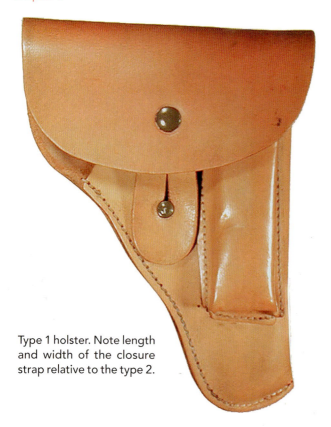

rear of the body. New holsters fit vz. 50 pistols snugly, closing with only minor stretching. (Photographs of a ČZ 27 pistol offered for sale with a natural pigskin leather holster that appeared to be a type 1 have been observed, but the holster was shown with its flap closed and it was impossible to be certain of its type. Since some vz. 52 holsters made during the same period utilized pigskin leather, it is reasonable to assume that the same material was used on vz. 50 holsters, but if so, they are much less common than cowhide.)

Type 1 holster. Note length and width of the closure strap relative to the type 2.

Type 2 holster produced for the vz. 27. *Alan J. Bell collection*

114   The ČZ Models 50 and 70

A composite holster, classified as the **type 2**, was made of a double layer of dark-green cotton fabric with a dark-brown pebble-grain cowhide leather magazine pouch, closure strap, belt loop, border trim, and reinforcement around the closure stud. Skramouššký and Badalík (1996, 252) indicate that it was produced both for the vz. 27 and the vz. 50, although it is not clear whether, like the transitional holster, it was first produced for the vz. 27 and later expanded to accommodate the vz. 50. Its classification was based on a similar composite holster produced for the vz. 52 army pistol after its leather holster had been standardized, but it may actually predate the type 1. Dimensions on the specimen shown match those of Communist-era vz. 27 holsters and the leather used is similar to early postwar holsters, indicating that this specimen predated the vz. 50. In spite of its double thickness, the fabric did not wear well and most holsters of this type were discarded, making specimens extremely difficult to find.

The **type 3** holster, pictured by Skramoušský and Badalík (1996, 253), is similar to the type 1 except that its closure strap is teardrop shaped to strengthen it around the stud hole and the edges of the flap, closure strap, and magazine pouch are lightly welted. The belt loop is stitched at the top and bottom, but

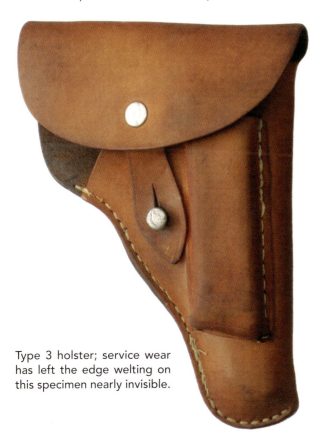

Type 3 holster; service wear has left the edge welting on this specimen nearly invisible.

World War II German WaA668-marked supplemental vz. 27 holster, closed (*above*) and open

Czech Cold War Police Pistols 115

Chapter 8

the top may be reinforced with rivets. It may simply have been an interpretation of the type 1 design by a different manufacturer, but the absence of markings makes this impossible to determine.

The **type 4** holster was originally developed for use with the vz. 27 by the Germans during World War II as a supplement (not a replacement) for the standard design, which remained in production through the end of the war. The reason for its development is unclear, although its shape may have been intended to better utilize residual scraps of leather left over from the manufacture of other products; it could also have been thought that its closure strap arrangement, which opens with a downward stroke of the hand, was superior to the traditional arrangement which opens with an upward stroke. Surviving specimens are scarce and are often confused with postwar Czech holsters made for the vz. 50, using the same design. The wartime holster is made of 6-ounce natural, full-grain, split-cowhide leather; the body and flap are made from a single piece. The flap is 134 mm wide at the fold, the closed holster is 172 mm long top to toe, and the open holster is 257 mm long; its magazine pouch is 100 mm long, with a perpendicular top edge. The closure strap is attached to the body with a steel rivet and is 90 mm long, with both ends rounded; a steel closure stud is attached to the flap and padded on the inside with a 30 mm leather patch (missing from the author's specimen, although its outline remains visible). Stitching utilizes white thread. Edge welting is present on the body, flap, and magazine pouch. A single 47 mm wide belt loop is sewn to the rear of the body. The inside of the flap is ink-stamped,

Nur für Pistole 27(t)
Kal. 7.65 m.m.

The outside of the flap carries a **WaA668** stamp just below the fold, an inspection mark associated with a number of different makers in Offenbach a.M., including Maury & Co. (1943) and R. Conte (1944). It fits the vz. 27 comfortably but will not accept a vz. 50 without stretching.

Postwar Czech holsters of this design were made for the vz. 50 and are found in subtypes **a** and **b**; the **type 4a** is pictured by Skramoušský and Badalík (1996, 254). It is made of 6-ounce buffed, natural, split-cowhide leather; the closed holster is 138 mm wide at the fold and 185 mm long, while the open

Type 4a holster with edge welting, rounded closure strap rivet end, and unfinished rivet

Type 4b holster shows edge welting only on the magazine pouch and has a square rivet end to the closure strap and a blackened steel rivet.

holster is 270 mm long. The magazine pouch is 100 mm long, with a perpendicular top opening. The closure strap is attached to the body with an unfinished steel rivet and is 96 mm long, with both ends rounded; a steel closure stud is attached to the flap and may be unprotected or padded with a leather patch sewn or glued to the inside of the flap. The single belt loop is 50 mm wide; edge welting on the flap, closure strap, magazine pouch, and belt loop may be present or absent. All observed specimens are unmarked.

The **type 4b** is identical except for the closure strap, which is 90 mm long with its upper end rounded and its lower end cut square; the body rivet is blackened and the closure stud is padded with a leather patch sewn onto the inside of the flap. Unlike other early vz. 50 holsters, it may be unmarked or ink-stamped **K6 ⚔ 64** inside the flap.

A "half flap" belt holster identified as the **vz. 62** was adopted in 1962 and was produced in small numbers but was never actually issued (Jan Balkar, personal communication); it is considered rare today, although a few have been offered for sale on internet auction sites at modest prices. It is made from 6-ounce buffed, natural, top-grain, split-cowhide leather, 208 mm long and 82 mm wide, with a single 50 × 42 mm belt loop sewn to its rear that will accept belts up to 1 inch wide. Stitching utilizes white thread. It has a thumb-break top snap closure and a short strap with snap with no known function is fastened

Vz. 62 holster for the vz. 50 pistol

Czech Cold War Police Pistols

Chapter 8

to its front; it does not restrain the pistol and unsnapping it detaches it from the holster. The half flap covers only the pistol's hammer and grip tang and is not effective; the pistol can be pulled slightly to the rear and drawn without unsnapping it and may fall out when its wearer is running or moving actively, explaining its rejection. This holster may be unmarked or carry an **OTK** ink stamp; its maker is unknown.

The **type 5** holster was made for the VB (Veřejné bezpečnosti, Public Safety Police, the uniformed branch of the SNB) and first appeared in photos taken during the 1968 Prague Spring uprising; it soon became the standard belt holster for most uniformed Czech police and was widely exported. The standard version is made from 4-ounce buffed, top-grain, split-cowhide leather dyed dark brown on the outside, with brown- or black-painted or unpainted rivets and a spare magazine pouch formed by an extension of the holster body below the pistol's butt. Stitching on the standard version utilizes dark-brown thread, while the dress versions use white thread. Twin belt loops extend above the flap, making the holster ride below the belt; the closure strap is riveted to the flap. Early specimens are unmarked, while later ones are ink-stamped **K6** ✕ with 70s to early 90s dates on the inside of the flap and may include the Kozak name and factory location in Delní Beřkovice. The holster is 146 mm wide at the fold, 190 mm long top to toe closed (excluding the belt loops), and 247 mm long open. Early holsters have plain flaps but beginning in 1974 an extra layer of leather was stitched to the inside of the flap, strengthening it. The dress version was made in three variations; the first is dimensionally identical to the standard model but is made of pigskin leather faced with white vinyl

Type 5 holsters, showing early unlined flap (*top*) and later lined flap

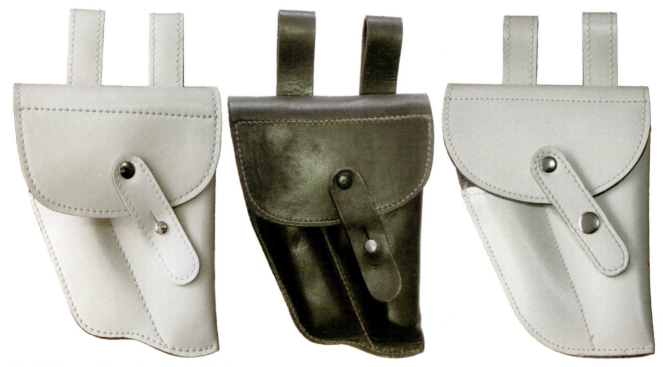

Type 5 holsters, *left to right*: standard, leather dress, and synthetic dress; snap closure variant of synthetic dress holster shown

The ČZ Models 50 and 70

Holsters and Accessories

and has nickel plated rivets, a stud-and-strap closure, and similar markings and dates. The second version is made of synthetic fabric faced with white vinyl and is cut differently at the toe, with nickel-plated rivets and a stud-and-strap closure. The third version is similar to the second with the closure stud replaced by a snap, since it is too stiff to accept a stud. The synthetic holsters may be unmarked or carry 70s to early 80s dates, and they lack the elasticity of leather; the author's specimens will not close over a pistol and while there are photos of Czech police officers wearing them, it is questionable whether they were actually used to carry pistols.

An open-top metropolitan police holster was also produced for the vz. 50-70, probably to replace the failed vz. 62, using 6-ounce top-grain, black-cowhide leather, dyed black, molded and stiffened with a steel shank to raise the pistol's butt; it has a thumb-break snap closure strap. It was made in right- and left-handed versions and is 180 mm long and 92 mm wide. Its rear is embossed with the trademark of Žílí/Praha, the encircled ČZ logo, and the model designation 50/70. This holster offers no protection for the pistol's grip, probably accounting for the extensive wear often seen on the rear corner of the right grip panels of police surplus vz. 70s.

Open-topped Czech shoulder holster produced for the StB

Open-top metropolitan police hip holster, left- and right-handed

Several types of shoulder holsters were made for the vz. 50-70. Czech holsters produced for the StB (Státni bezpečnost, State Security Police, the undercover branch of the SNB) are open topped and made of 4-ounce natural, buffed, top-grain, split-cowhide leather, either plain or embossed in a diamond "fish-scale" pattern often applied to Czech Cold War–era military leather goods. The author's specimen of the embossed type is ink-stamped **K6 ⚔ 74** on the inside of the closure strap, while the plain specimens are ink-stamped **K6 ⚔ 76** and **KOZAK, n. p. Dolní Beřkovice / OTK c. 1 rok výroby 1991**, respectively. The closure straps have two fastening notches but only the lower one is usable, since

Czech Cold War Police Pistols   119

Chapter 8

Undercover belt holster and magazine pouch produced for the StB; pouch snaps may be painted either black or tan.

fastening the other effectively folds the rear of the holster over the front. The bodies are 180 mm long and 117 mm wide; all harness straps are leather and are attached by steel loops to leather tabs that are riveted to the body. The same holster body and closure strap, minus the harness and with an extra layer of leather sewn into the top half and two vertical belt slots cut in the rear, were also produced for the StB as an undercover belt holster; one of the author's specimens is unmarked, while the other is ink-stamped on the inside of the closure strap, **KOZAK, n. p. Dolní Beřkovice / OTK c. 2 rok výroby 1973**. A separate belt pouch for a spare magazine was issued with these holsters; it is 43 mm wide and 117 mm long, with a snap closure and the top and bottom contoured to match a plain-base magazine (it will not accept finger-rest magazines). Closure snaps may be painted tan or dark brown, or they may be unpainted bright metal; the author's specimen is ink-stamped **K6 / 75** on the inside of the flap. (The StB shoulder and belt holsters are extremely tight and must be moistened and stretched to accept a vz. 50-70; this may have been done to allow their use with the 6.35 mm vz. 45, which they also accommodate.)

A less frequently seen vz. 50-70 shoulder holster has a 4-ounce open-top, natural, split-cowhide leather body that is 140 mm wide and 180 mm long, with a 65 mm long buttonhole tab at its toe; the top of the body has an extra layer of reinforcing leather stitched to it with two 18 mm slots for the harness. Instead of a closure strap, a retaining strap that wraps around the pistol's grip is riveted to the body, with a closure snap similar to the one on the single magazine pouch described above. Stitching utilizes white thread. The shoulder harness is made of 20 mm wide white cotton webbing, with a leather adjustment slide and keeper and a slotted leather tab with two buttonholes for belt attachment; there is no provision for a spare magazine. This holster fits vz. 50-70s comfortably without stretching; the author's specimen is unmarked but carried a Czech paper tag with the stock number and an ink-stamped inspector's name. A belt version of this holster was also produced, with two belt loops sewn to its rear; the author has been unable to obtain a specimen to measure and photograph.

A shoulder version of the vz. 62 holster was produced but apparently carried no model designation (Jan Balcar, personal communication); it was widely used by plainclothes police officers but was disliked because its harness was uncomfortable and produced a visible outline on the wearer's jacket, making it difficult to conceal. Its body is similar in shape and size to the belt holster and has a partial flap that covers the pistol's hammer and grip tang, but it is riveted in place without a thumb-break snap. A snap closure strap around the trigger guard effectively retains the pistol. Its leather harness is attached with laces and slots, allowing size adjustments, and it has elastic cotton-webbing straps with clasps to attach it and the holster toe to the wearer's trousers. The author's specimen carries an ink-stamped **OTK** mark on the inside of the harness and **60** within a square on the inside of the closure strap.

Other shoulder holsters associated with the vz. 50-70 have 4-ounce natural, top-grain, split-cowhide leather bodies, a variety of leather or vinyl closure straps or flaps, and a white cotton-webbing shoulder harness with leather keepers. A separate leather spare-magazine pouch is usually attached to the harness or holster body but accepts only

Holsters and Accessories

Open-top vz. 50-70 shoulder holster with cotton-webbing harness, snap closure retaining strap, and Czech identification tag

Shoulder version of the vz. 62 holster

plain-base magazines. Vinyl closure flaps may be white, yellow, or orange; a variety of ink-stamped markings have been observed that do not appear to be Czech and suggest that the holsters were produced in East Germany.

South Africa produced cotton-webbing vz. 50-70 holsters for its defense force (SADF) and police (SAP), designed for use with pattern 70 and 73 belts and field gear. SADF holsters are OD green, 8" long top to toe, 4⅛" wide, and open topped and open toed, with separate straps and snap closures for the pistol pocket and magazine pouch and fit vz. 50-70s and similar-sized pistols snugly; they were used in the 1966–88 "Angola Bush War" against Cuban-backed Southwest African People's Organization (SWAPO) insurgents in what is now Namibia. SAP holsters are blue, 7⅝" long, and 4¼" wide, with double-snap straps to accommodate a variety of pistols; their slightly wider pockets will accept

Shoulder holster for vz. 50-70 with spare magazine carrier and cotton-webbing harness; probably made in East Germany

Czech Cold War Police Pistols

121

Chapter 8

South African Defense Force and South African Police cotton-webbing belt holsters for the vz. 50-70; the police holster has a slightly wider body and double closure snaps to fit a variety of pistols.

Cleaning brushes furnished with vz. 50-70s

.38-caliber Enfield, Webley, and K-frame Smith & Wesson revolvers with barrel lengths up to 5". Larger cotton-webbing holsters, 12¾" long and 4" wide with a full flap closure, spare-magazine and cleaning-rod pouches, and an attached ammunition pouch, were produced for SADF and SAP use with M-1935 Browning pistols.

A 135 mm long soft-bristle cleaning brush with a twisted wire handle was supplied with each vz. 50-70. Its bristle-bearing section is 15 mm in diameter and 65 mm long and was probably intended for use on the inside of the magazine rather than the pistol's bore, which can be cleaned more effectively with a .32-caliber bronze brush. No other tools made for use with these pistols are known, although steel cleaning rods for the vz. 52 army pistol are often erroneously advertised as "original" vz. 50-70 rods.

Early vz. 50 commercial box serial number 663992 (*above*), damaged and repaired with tape; box end (*below*) with Thalson Company import label

122   The ČZ Models 50 and 70

Commercial vz. 50s produced at Strakonicé were shipped in light-gray cardboard boxes that are 175 mm long, 130 mm wide, and 32 mm deep; the top carries a black line drawing of a vz. 50 pistol with the prototype slide legend (no slide-gripping grooves are shown), a 40 mm encircled ČZ logo in the lower left corner, and the pistol's serial number in 10 mm characters ink-stamped in the upper right corner. The figures on the box top are printed on a paper wrapper that is glued around it, securing the corners; the sides of the bottom are also paper-covered, but the underside is bare except at the edges. The sides of the top have 20 mm diameter semicircular finger recesses to allow the bottom to be grasped for opening and the box has no interior liner; the author's specimen, which is brittle from age, acid content, and less-than-ideal storage conditions, has been crudely repaired with tape. It carries the label of the US importer Thalson Company of San Francisco, glued upside down on one end and included an English-language copy of the early instruction manual (Thalson also imported post-war vz. 27 and vz. 45 pistols). It is not known whether government contract vz. 50s were also packed in these boxes; they may have been packed in plain paper boxes or multipistol wooden chests.

Boxes issued with pistols produced at ZUB prior to 1968 are tan or gray in color without decoration; they are rare and the author has been unable to obtain a specimen to measure and photograph. Boxes of this type may have continued to be used with vz. 50s and vz. 70s consigned to Czech municipal police departments, since these pistols have been offered for sale with similar boxes, but they may have been provided by importers rather than the factory. In early 1968 (lowest observed serial number C31452), a redesigned box was introduced that is 197 mm long, 135 mm wide, and 32 mm deep, with a white bottom and a dark-blue-and-white top, bearing a picture of a pistol, the ČZ logo, caliber, model 50 designation, and national origin. Like the early commercial box, a printed paper wrapper is glued over the cardboard top; the sides and underside of the bottom are covered with a white paper wrapper. A paper sticker on one end labeled "Výrobní číslo" carries the hand-inscribed serial number, with or without prefix; boxes are occasionally observed with the serial number inscribed directly on the box end, without a sticker. (When reading hand-inscribed Czech serial numbers, note that 1s always have downward-angled serifs at the top left and 7s always have horizontal crossbars.) The interior of the box holds a cardboard liner with the ČZ logo, cutouts for the pistol and cleaning brush, two sheets of

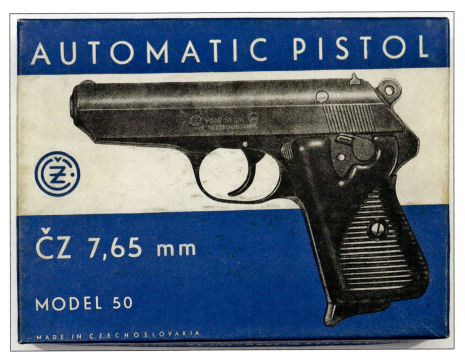

Vz. 50 pistol box introduced in 1968

Factory stamp and hand-inscribed serial number on bottom of 1968 box C33603 (*above*); box end with label on box D94501 (*below*).

Chapter 8

Vz. 50-70 pistol box interior with pistol and cleaning brush

Table 8-1		Observed Pistol Boxes during Transition
Serial Number	Date	Box type
195308	74	70 late
199710	74	50
199777	74	50
199885	74	50
200041	74	70 early
200112	74	70 late
200116	74	70 late
200122	74	70 late
200271	74	50
200353	74	70 late
200492	74	70 late
200575	74	70 late
200769	74	50
200820	74	50
200836	74	50
202043	74	70 early
202050	74	70 late
202065	74	70 late
202487	74	70 late
202580	74	70 late
202610	74	70 early
202658	74	70 early
202677	74	70 early
203020	74	70 late
204581	75	70 early

chemically treated paper for rust protection, and an 8¼" × 12" factory test target; it is not known when the practice of including test targets with the pistols began, but 65-dated serial number B69224 came with one and it is likely that they were added either at the start of production at ZUB in 1957 or at the restart in 1964. Vz. 50 marked targets were used on pistols of both models through 1983. The targets have the pistol's serial number hand-inscribed on a line marked **ČISLO PISTOLE** in the upper right corner and spaces for the test date (**DATUM**), shooter (**STŘELEC**), and inspector (**OTK**) to be ink-stamped at the bottom. The names of two shooters, Miloš and Zemek, appear on most observed targets from 1968 through 1981, the latest-dated target examined; one 1981 target has been observed with the name Fibichr. The inspector's stamp is often illegible, but **TK** over **100**, **172**, **195**, and **261** have been observed. Very early boxes of this type lack the serial number sticker; the number is hand-inscribed on one corner of the bottom, which also carries a 27 × 70 mm factory ink stamp.

Holsters and Accessories

Boxes for the vz. 70 were introduced in April 1971 at about serial number J07400 (with considerable overlapping), but were discontinued in January 1972 due to problems with the illustration; the earliest observed serial number is J07471 and the highest is J73445. Vz. 50 boxes were again used from January 1972 until late 1974, when a second vz. 70 box was introduced at about serial number 195000. At that time, a decision was apparently made to use up leftover stocks of vz. 50 and early vz. 70 paper wrappers to make boxes and for at least two months all three box types were produced and issued at random; a sample of boxes from this period is presented in table 8-1. The full length of the transition period has not been determined, but after early 1975 all vz. 70s were issued in late-type boxes. Early vz. 70 boxes have white bottoms and pale-blue tops including a picture of the left side of a vz. 70 (actually a vz. 69 with its modified safety lever), with the pistol's nomenclature and the ČZ logo on the lower left corner; some early boxes have a 1 mm white outline around the edge of the top, but this is uncommon. The box sides carry the pistol's nomenclature and national origin, while the ends carry the number of shots and caliber. Late vz. 70 boxes are the same color with identical side and end markings, but the top pictures the right side of a vz. 70 with the nomenclature and ČZ logo on the lower right corner. Both types have interior inserts and serial number stickers similar to vz. 50 boxes, although the size of the stickers varied slightly over time; the star prefix used on MV pistols beginning in 1976 and triangle prefix used on most other pistols beginning in 1979 are not used on the box serial numbers. Color intensity varies on both types of vz. 70 boxes.

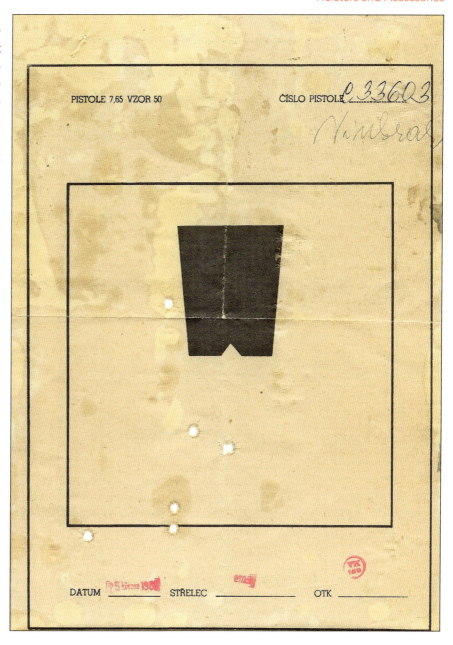

Test target issued with vz. 50 serial number C33603, dated 25 March 1968. Vz. 50 targets were used until the end of vz. 70 production.

A 6" × 8" monofold promotional brochure for the vz. 50 was printed by Omnipol, ČZ's international distributer in Prague, probably before the start of production on the basis of the illustration, which shows a pistol with the prototype slide legend and features. The front is white with an image of the pistol and a green-and-yellow vertical stripe bearing the ČZ logo over a target at the top and the terms **EVER READY / ACCURATE / RELIABLE / SAFE** and the label **ČZ-7.65 / MOD. 50** at the bottom. The interior contains four paragraphs of text amplifying the terms on the front, while the back lists technical data along with the Omnipol logo.

Czech Cold War Police Pistols

Chapter 8

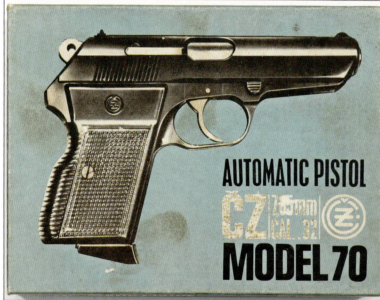

Vz. 70 pistol boxes, early (*above*) and late types

Two instruction manuals were printed for the vz. 50. Neither is dated but the first was evidently printed in 1950, since a copy was included in the commercial box pictured above that accompanied 1950 vz. 50 serial number 663992. It carries the label "Česká Zbrojovka Národní Podník" and was published at Strakonicé. It is titled *SAMMOČINA PISTOLE ČZ RÁŽE 7,65 mm, VZOR 50* (Semiautomatic Pistol ČZ Caliber 7.65 mm, Model 50) and is 113 × 155 mm, with a black cover bearing a white outline drawing of the pistol with a red 35 mm ČZ logo on the front and a similar logo and a red-bordered white label for the distributor's identification on the rear. It contains thirty-two pages describing the ČZ company, the pistol, and its function and disassembly, along with parts diagrams and nomenclature; illustrations show pistols with prototype and first-variation markings. It was printed in the Czech, English, French, German, and Spanish languages.

The second manual is labeled *Přesné Strojírenství národní podnik Uherský Brod* and was published by ZUB. It is 138 × 138 mm, with a blue-bordered white cover, the front showing the ČZ logo, a hand holding a vz. 50 pistol with features indicating mid-1967 production, and the title *NÁVOD NA POUŽITÍ A ÚDRŽBU PISTOLE ČZ MODEL 50 RÁŽE 7,65 mm* (Instructions for Use and Maintenance [of the] Pistol ČZ Model 50 Caliber 7.65 mm), while the back shows only a picture of the pistol. It contains ten pages with a more abbreviated description of the pistol and its operation, disassembly, and technical data, as well as a parts diagram. It was also printed in Czech, English, French, German, and Spanish.

Omnipol also produced a larger (8" × 8¼") six-page brochure for the vz. 50 that includes similar information and a foldout on the last page showing parts and nomenclature. The front cover carries the pistol's identification and the phrase "Pistol ČZ 7.65 a perfect weapon of Czechoslovak manufacture" above a photo of a hand holding the pistol, while the rear is dark green with the Omnipol address and trademark and a whimsical drawing of a man's head topped by a red apple with a bullet hole through it. The author's specimen is printed in English, but it was probably offered in the same languages as the smaller brochure.

A manual for the vz. 70 was also produced at ZUB; the author's specimen has an orange cover with a picture of a hand holding a vz. 70 pistol (with the vz. 69 safety lever) and the title in French, *INSTRUCTIONES D'EMPLOI ET D'ENTRETIEN DE PISTOLE ČZ MODÈLE 70 CALIBRE 7,75 mm (.32)*, over a large, stylized ČZ logo. It is the same size and follows the same format as the blue-and-white ZUB vz. 50 manual, but with pictures of the updated

126   The ČZ Models 50 and 70

Holsters and Accessories

Early monofold promotional brochure

First vz. 50 instruction manual, from Strakonicé

Large Omnipol brochure, front and rear covers

pistol; the parts diagram is expanded to show the slide and receiver with their components and nomenclature on separate pages, along with the Omnipol logo and address. The last page carries the same picture of a vz. 70 used on the late vz. 70 box; this manual was also published in Czech, English, German, and Spanish. Although sized to fit the pistol boxes, the manuals were not generally included in them but were provided to sales outlets and importers for distribution. *Famous Automatic Pistols and Revolvers, Volume 2*, compiled by John Olson and printed by Jolex Inc. in 1976, provides English text on pages 74–75 that was evidently extracted from this manual.

Turkish walnut display boxes for the vz. 50 are produced by Klinsky & Co., SRO (klinsky.cz) in the Czech Republic; the firm also produces fine-quality wooden pistol grips. The boxes have dovetailed sliding lids that are laser-engraved with the encircled ČZ logo, the company name and location used during Strakonicé production, and the national origin; CNC-machined spaces are provided for the

Czech Cold War Police Pistols

Chapter 8

Second vz. 50 instruction manual, from ZUB

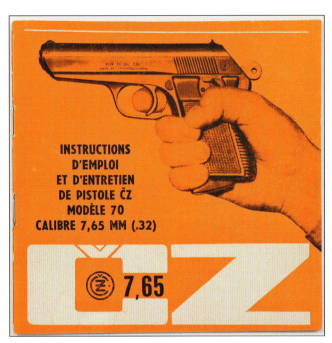
Vz. 70 manual from ZUB, French language

pistol, its magazine, and eight cartridges. The author's specimen has finely figured wood, measures 192 × 134 × 41 mm, and cost $115 in 2016. It fits vz. 50s (with magazine removed) but will not accept a vz. 70 due to the slightly increased depth of its trigger guard. The lid was a bit tight where it rides over the magazine base, evidently because the thickness of the velvet lining was not considered in its design, but this was remedied with judicious use of a Dremel tool.

The author also purchased a sample pair of Klinsky walnut grips for $69.95 on eBay.com, which came with a matching grip screw since the recess for the screwhead is too small to fit an original screw. A pair of steel indexing pins in the rear grip strap area ensure alignment of the two halves and while the packaging warned that some fitting might be necessary, a light reaming of the screw hole in the left panel was all that was necessary for a snug fit. Contours match original vz. 50 grip panels (without the muzzle-raising change incorporated in vz. 70 grips), but overall thickness is slightly increased and there is a small thumb rest on both sides. The lower half of each panel is checkered and the author found the resulting grip to be firm and comfortable.

Klinsky Turkish walnut display box for the vz. 50

A tan-colored, limited-edition, 9¼" × 6" × 1½" Kraft paper display/shipping box, produced by Cylinder & Slide, Inc., 245 East 4th Street, Fremont, Nebraska, 66025, (402) 721-4277, was introduced in 2020 at a price of $54.95. The box top carries the encircled ČZ logo, ČESKÁ ZBROJOVKA company name, and an illustration from the 1950 manual showing a full-sized artist's rendition of a vz. 50 with prototype markings, not the line drawing used on the original commercial box. The maker's identification is ink-stamped on the inside of the box top and bottom. It is well made, with graphics sealed for protection, and includes a folded sheet of acid-free brown waxed paper for a lining. It is suited for the purposes described but should not be mistaken for an original; due to its size, internal padding would be needed if it is used for shipping.

The Czech SNB was a paramilitary organization, with uniforms identical to those of the Czech army except for red hatbands and shoulder boards that identified them as police; most SNB officers were also members of the Czech Communist Party. Service and achievement decorations similar to military medals and badges were awarded, and

Klinsky vz. 50-70 walnut grip panels

SNB-marked Czech handcuffs, made by Ralk in 1949

Kraft paper Cylinder & Barrel vz. 50 shipping and display box

Chapter 8

there were separate police and "police helper" (Pomocná stráž Veřejné bezpečnosti, or PSVB) badges worn by criminal, municipal, and socialist police units not directly connected to the SNB. These decorations, along with police-marked equipment, party credentials, and uniform components, are often offered for sale on internet websites. While not directly associated with vz. 50-70 pistols, they add context, depth, and interest to a collection and are worthy of consideration.

Czech Criminal Service numbered police badge from the 1950s

Dress uniform hat and shoulder boards of a SNB *poručíku* (second lieutenant); the heart-shaped linden leaves on the SNB shoulder board insignia are a Czech national symbol.

Medals and badges awarded to SNB *kapitán* (captain), later major, Slavomil Kerbr: 30 Years' Service (1975), SNB Badge (a replacement, Výměna, 1976), SNB Medal (1979), and 40th Year of Liberation Honorary Medal (undated, 1985)

Holsters and Accessories

SNB Honorary Badge awarded to Nadporučíku (First Lieutenant) Antonínu Vičkovi, 1970

VZORNY KOLEKTIV (exemplary team) SNB badges, awarded in gold, silver, and bronze levels

Gold-level Exemplary Team ZNB badge (Slovak language)

Boxed 70 mm bronze "table medal" for service in federal administration of the SNB Public Security Police, with an image of Prague Castle, built in the ninth century

Municipal police patches from Plzen, Usti Nad Labem, Kladno, Liberec, Praha (Prague), and Most. These patches usually display coats of arms or local landmarks reflecting the rich cultural heritage of the Czech people.

Czech Cold War Police Pistols

131

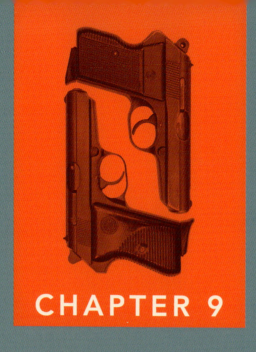

CHAPTER 9

Valuation

This subject is tricky, because values are fluid and a value estimate is merely a snapshot through a particular window in time. The law of supply and demand can readjust unexpectedly if a government agency modernizes and dumps its inventory of older pistols onto the surplus market, producing a flurry of potential bargains on variants that had previously been nearly unobtainable. Large numbers of these pistols were imported in the 1990s and first few years of the 2000s; they were commonly seen at gun shows and on internet auction sites but little was known about them and prices were quite modest. Although small lots continue to be imported, they have become more difficult to find and prices have risen accordingly. Inflation is also a significant factor; most values provided are based on 2021–22 prices, but if the federal government continues its current practice of unbridled printing of paper currency without foundational value, they will become meaningless except as a relative index. In the past, values of vz. 50-70 pistols have been based primarily on their utility as modest-sized defense weapons with relatively little historical significance; information on variations and their numbers was not widely available and few collectors showed interest in them, although that is changing as the Cold War generation matures and interest in its arms and artifacts increases. The database indicates that there are considerably more vz. 70s than vz. 50s in circulation in the US but this is not generally reflected in pricing, which depends more on condition than actual scarcity. Commercial vz. 50s from Strakonicé are more difficult to find than NB-marked pistols, but this is not widely known and has little influence on pricing. Pistols retaining most of their original finish currently bring $300–$350, while those with more extensive wear are more likely to sell for prices in the $150–$250 range. Those offered for $400 or more often remain unsold for extended periods unless they are accompanied by original boxes or have unusual features that attract collector attention. However, there are surprises; one NB 50–marked pistol that had been rebuilt and proof-dated 80, accompanied by a second magazine and a Makarov holster and cleaning rod, was offered as a "complete rig" on GunBroker.com in 2021, drew thirteen bids, and sold for $790 (the bidders who drove the price up were probably unaware that the holster and rod did not match the pistol). Original boxes and other accessories increase marketing appeal; the author has observed that vz. 70s in "as new" condition with original boxes and test targets sell for as much as $700, but this is unusual; prices above $450 for such pieces usually meet some resistance and they sell rather slowly. (Two "as new" vz. 70s with original boxes and targets offered on GunBroker.com in

Valuation

74-dated vz. 70 serial number 200041 with its original "early" vz. 70 box and test target, sold for $425 on GunBroker.com in 2020

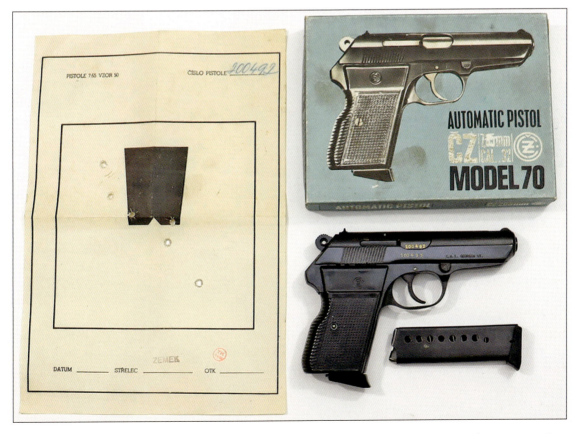

74-dated vz. 70 serial number 200492 with its original "late" vz. 70 box, test target, and extra magazine, sold for $465 on GunBroker.com in 2021

Chapter 9

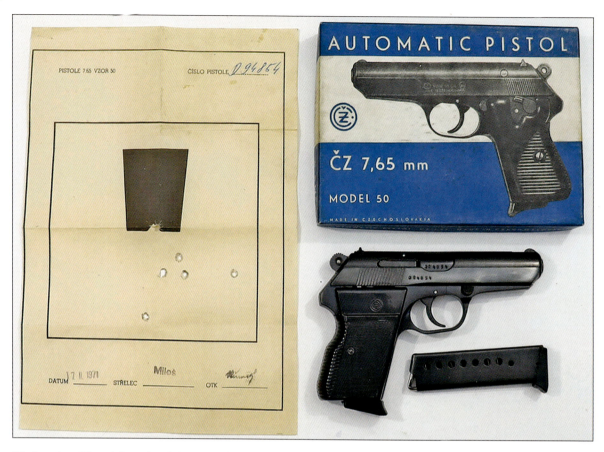

71-dated vz. 70 serial number D94854 with its original vz. 50 box, test target, and extra magazine, in immaculate condition, is not import marked and was undoubtedly purchased in Europe and brought home by a US diplomat or military service member stationed there. It sold for $727 on GunBroker.com in 2022.

January 2022 brought only $327 and $347, respectively, but the auctions were of short duration with no reserve and offering them simultaneously diminished potential competition, undoubtedly suppressing the prices.) Nickel plating usually does not increase a pistol's value unless it is original and in immaculate condition; flaked or peeling plating downgrades value more than similar wear on blued pistols. If the serial numbers and other stamped markings do not display "cratering"—slightly raised rims of displaced metal around the edges of the impressions that can be felt with a fingertip—the surface has almost certainly been polished, and the plating is not original. Another quick check is the dimple below the safety lever on the left side of the receiver; if it does not contain a spot of red paint, the plating is not factory work.

As an experiment, when a scarce variant was offered for sale at a modest price on GunBroker.com in 2016, the author contacted the seller and provided information to add to the item description, correctly identifying the variant and its scarcity. The result was a dramatic increase in bidding and a final sale price of $655—on a pistol that had previously sold for about $250. This illustrates the potential value of information on such pistols.

MS 50–marked serial number 675613, one of an estimated five hundred vz. 50s produced for the Czech Ministry of Justice

134   The ČZ Models 50 and 70

Valuation

50-dated serial number 693971, equipped with a prototype hammer, is a candidate for restoration but would require polishing to remove surface damage before refinishing.

80-dated serial number ☆617981 is the highest-known star prefix vz. 70.

Czech Cold War Police Pistols

Appraised values are normally based on recent comparable sales, but such data are not currently available for most scarce variants because they have not been offered to an "informed" market; many of the figures presented here are thus based on their rates of occurrence in the database. MS 50–marked vz. 50s should command a substantial premium because of their rarity; only six specimens are known, all from the first marking variation, and while the exact number produced has not been released, mathematical analysis of their rate of occurrence in the serial number range where they are found, compared to the rates of occurrence of other vz. 50s within that range, indicates that the number was probably five hundred. This should peg the value of fine specimens over $750, with prices in the $600 range for pistols with more finish wear. (Most of these pistols were exposed to only modest use in Czech service, but their treatment after importation to the US is unpredictable.) 1952 commercial vz. 50s are rare in the US, occurring at about the same rate as MS 50s in the database; since they are unlikely to reappear on surplus markets in meaningful numbers, they should command similar prices. Aluminum-grip vz. 50s are also rare, although their non-Czech origin makes them more of an oddity, as noted above; one in excellent condition drew forty-seven bids at auction in 2017 and sold for $342, while the author paid $255 for serial number D67329 in 2021. However, that pistol's grips had been given a sloppy coat of black spray paint and it is unlikely that other potential buyers recognized them. Prototype hammer vz. 50s occur at a slightly higher rate, suggesting numbers of about 750 and prices of $500–$600 in fine condition. Star prefix vz. 70s occur at a slightly higher rate than prototype hammers (there are sixteen in the database), although their numbers in the US are clearly not representative of actual production and future imports could significantly increase availability; a price of $500 for a fine specimen might be fair, but somewhat risky. Strakonicé vz. 50s rebarreled and reproofed prior to 1979 occur with enough frequency to be considered a distinct variant; their rate of appearance in the database suggests numbers around 2,500, but their status as oddities limits the number of collectors who would be willing to pay a premium for them. A well-written descriptive advertisement will probably spur bidder interest, but it would be surprising to see one bring much more than $100 above the expected price for the same pistol in

Serial number B31710, a scarce vz. 50 produced in 1960, is an excellent candidate for restoration, since it has a good deal of finish wear but no pitting or other metal damage.

original condition. Government contract vz. 50s rebuilt and refinished for commercial sale in 1979–82 are also of limited collector interest but the rebuilding may actually detract from their value if original markings are impaired by refinishing, so the pistols lack the appeal of originality.

Rare dates are always interesting to collectors; 510 pistols were reportedly produced in 1957, only 171 in 1963, and 425 in 1983, giving these dates special appeal. The author has never seen vz. 50-70s with these dates offered for sale so any value estimate would be unsupported, but they would certainly merit careful description and marketing to as large an audience as possible. In 1960, there were 2,001 vz. 50s produced in approximately the B30510–B32510 serial range and to date, the author has seen only two marketed, the first with its last two serial digits obscured; at the time, its scarcity was not recognized, its condition was unimpressive, and the author let it pass without a bid. The second, B31710, is far from pristine and was purchased for $300 without competition in 2021, probably because no other potential bidders recognized its scarcity (it has no pitting, only holster wear, making it an excellent candidate for restoration). A few other 60 dates would be expected to have turned up after more than sixty years, but their fate remains unknown. Pazdera (2013) attributes the scarcity of specimens from early ZUB production to the fact that they were "exported to rather tumultuous corners of the globe." In 1982 there were 8,445 vz. 70s produced, but enough of them have appeared to satisfy interested collectors and blunt any significant pricing spike. B-series vz. 50s dated 65 and 66 are not rare but their occurrence in the database is sparse, suggesting that few have been imported into the US; careful marketing would again help boost their prices toward the $500 range. Vz. 70s dated 78 are scarce and those dated 77 and 79 are also difficult to find, making them worthy of special attention; all database records in the 300 000 through 500 000 serial range are sparse. Cardinal-numbered pistols (e.g., vz. 70 number 100000) are of interest to some collectors and would merit a modest premium if marketed skillfully.

The twenty-one-groove slide variant is something of an enigma. Only six specimens are known, one of them merely a stripped slide, all from a range of about 1,300 serial numbers with an apparent "cap" about 300 numbers above it. Below this range, serial numbers C01298, C00440, C00024, B99705, and

67-dated serial number C01562 with twenty-one-groove slide and solid hammer is also the earliest known specimen with the embossed wave pattern on the sighting rib.

B98503 have ring hammers and fifteen slide grooves, indication a "floor" about 250 numbers below the observed range. It is also possible that the fifteen-groove slide overlapped the lower end of the known twenty-one-groove range and the sixteen-groove slide overlapped its upper end, reducing the actual number of twenty-one-groove slides. It appears that this variant includes fewer than 2,000 pistols—perhaps a lot fewer—making it rare, but more data are needed to better define it. The only other clue is the artist's drawing that appears on the 1968 vz. 50 pistol box and instruction manual showing a pistol with fifteen slide grooves and a large-hole ring hammer, bolstering the idea that the ring hammer was in full production before the twenty-one-groove slide was introduced. The ring hammer would have required new tooling, while the change from fifteen to twenty-one slide grooves, which are assumed to have been cut by successive passes of a single tool, could have been accomplished by adjusting the existing machinery to cut six more grooves. To further complicate matters, there are subvariants with twenty-one-groove slides; serial numbers C01562, C01973, C02020, and C02861 have wave-pattern sighting ribs, while number C02239 has the earlier "smooth forged" rib. Both solid and ring hammers were used on twenty-one-groove pistols; C01562 is equipped with a solid hammer while the other complete specimens all have ring hammers, producing a second pair of subvariants. Any collector wishing to acquire one of these pistols can expect a long and perhaps fruitless search, but what should a seller ask for one? If Luger pistols were the subject these would be rare and valuable pieces, but we aren't playing in that ballpark; probably about the same price that would be expected for an MS 50, but a fine specimen, properly marketed, could bring considerably more if several collectors were bidding on it.

1967 vz. 50 serial numbers B99705 and C00024 bracket the B- to C-series change and illustrate the two subvariants of the scarce ring hammer with fifteen-groove slide variant.

Serial numbers B98503, B99705, C00024, C00440, and C01298 introduce yet another scarce variant, vz. 50s equipped with fifteen-groove slides and early ring hammers, also divided into two sub-variants from the late B and early C series. The earliest observed pistol with the ring hammer is serial number B98503, but as noted above, there is a significant data gap below it. Serial numbers B88460, B89259, B89756, B89923, and B92533 all are equipped with the solid hammer, indicating that it was still in use through April 1967, but number B98503 would probably have been accepted in June, leaving two months—about 6,000 serial numbers—in which the change could have occurred (plus possible overlapping), making it difficult to estimate the number of pistols that were equipped with ring hammers before the fifteen-groove slide was replaced by the twenty-one-groove version. (Solid hammers observed on early C-series pistols demonstrate that B98503, B99705, C00024, C00440, and C01298 were produced during the overlapping period of the hammer change.) This variant may not actually be rare but it is currently scarce in the US, with only the five records noted in the database. Since this version of the vz. 50 was chosen for the illustration on the box introduced in 1968 there are undoubtedly collectors who would be interested in acquiring a specimen, but its value is difficult to establish. B99705 was sold as one of a lot of three vz. 50 "repair/parts guns" in 2021 by Old Western Scrounger; the lot drew nineteen bids and the author bought it for $436, but it is unlikely that the other bidders recognized that pistol's potential value. The other two pistols in the sale were basically $100 parts guns, with defects that made them impractical to rebuild for sale, but B99705 arrived in surprisingly nice condition and was easily restored; it was apparently sidelined due to a frozen firing pin, which the person responsible for it did not know how to remedy. Serial number C00024 was offered in a fourteen-day auction on GunBroker.com in 2022 at a starting price of $295 and the author bought it without competition, evidently because no other collectors recognized its scarcity.

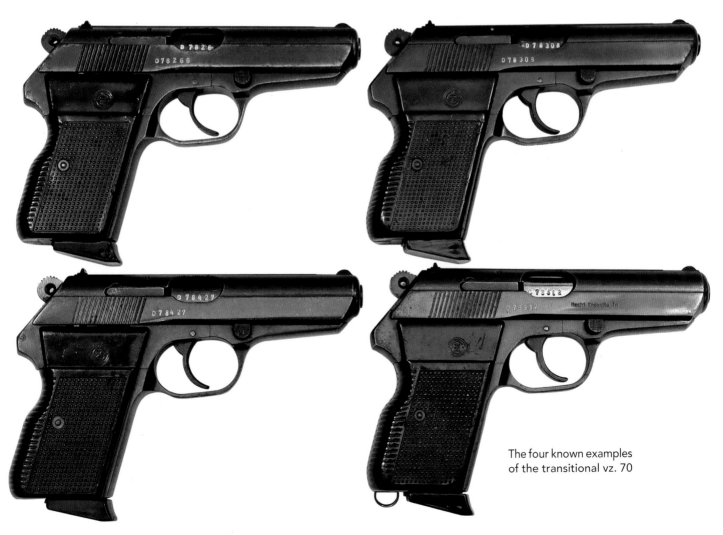

The four known examples of the transitional vz. 70

Another challenging subject is the "transitional" variant assembled during the vz. 70 model change, with a vz. 70 slide and furniture installed on a matching-numbered vz. 50 receiver. This variant was only recently confirmed to be more than a mere oddity, its numbers remain in question, and prior to the publication of this work its existence was known only by the author and a few of his contacts. (Mathematical analysis of the available data from the 78,000 serial block suggests that 333 transitionals might have been produced, but this is a very crude estimate; the clustering of known specimens and the interruption of the cluster by at least one normal vz. 50 argue against a quantity that large.) This variant is certainly interesting, and a specimen in fine condition, properly marketed, should attract significant collector attention; attempting to peg its value at this point involves a good bit of speculation, but it should be worth at least as much as an MS 50. Serial number D78266 is both a transitional variant and the earliest currently known vz. 70, although the latter distinction will probably change over time, but all four known specimens have finish wear or blemishes that could be detrimental to their market value; the only way to make a determination would be through carefully marketing one or more of them. The author has personally examined all four and can certify that they are genuine.

The author's specimens of the vz. 50 Sport pistol sold for about $500 each when offered for sale on GunBroker.com in 2019. Another Sport pistol sold for the equivalent of $600 on a Czech internet arms site at about the same time, validating the general price range. A Sport pistol was offered for sale on GunBroker.com in 2022 for $750 and sold for that price but drew only one bid; this is another little-known variant in the US that would benefit from an explanation of its purpose and history. Factory cutaway pistols, while rare, are also limited in interest to a relatively small number of collectors. The two known US specimens sold for $350–$500 in 2019 (the author paid a buy-it-now price for serial number X2001 to avoid the risk of losing it to another bidder), but the uniqueness and condition of both pistols probably suppressed their selling prices. It is possible that more specimens will be imported, perhaps in better condition, and they should be priced accordingly; a complete one in fine condition could bring as much as $1,000.

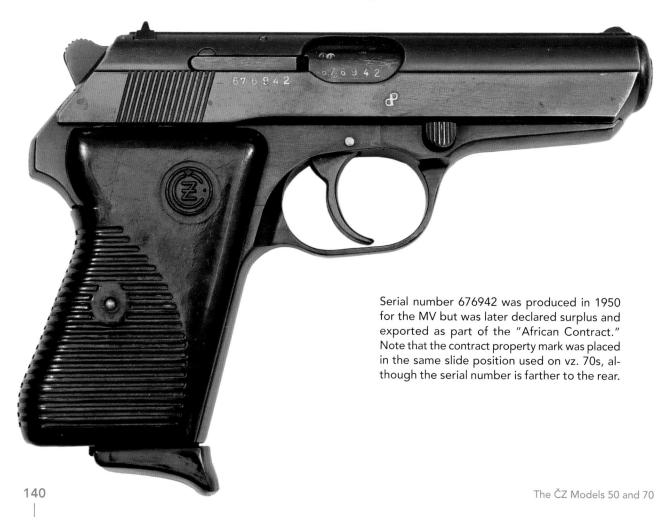

Serial number 676942 was produced in 1950 for the MV but was later declared surplus and exported as part of the "African Contract." Note that the contract property mark was placed in the same slide position used on vz. 70s, although the serial number is farther to the rear.

For advanced collectors, there are a few "sleepers" to look for. Because the model change to vz. 70 occurred both late in the year and late in the production of the D series, only about 7,100 70-dated D-series vz. 70s and 14,000 dated 71 were produced, making them difficult to find, especially in fine condition. A similar situation exists with very early 80-dated pistols, since implementation of the triangle serial prefix defining the sixth marking variation was completed in early 1980 and both 79-dated sixth-variation and 80-dated fifth-variation specimens are uncommon. Pistols dated 78 are currently uncommon in the US; although nearly 67,000 vz. 70s were produced that year, only twelve are recorded in the database. This is probably due to the large number of pistols that were delivered to the MV in that year and that later, after being declared surplus, were reportedly sold to a South American buyer; at some point they may reappear on the US surplus market, but that is unpredictable.

Unusual markings or other features may increase collector interest. African Contract vz. 70s are too common to qualify, but ⚔P-marked vz. 50s are scarce and thus potentially more valuable; only eight are recorded in the author's database. Other property or commercial markings may also increase interest, especially if they can be identified and linked to a pistol's history. Added proof marks, either Czech or from other nations, are noteworthy if they are unusual or connected to historical events. However, one should always be skeptical when unusual markings, features, or undocumented histories are a major component of a pistol's price, since fakery occurs even with relatively ordinary pistols such as the vz. 50-70. Specimens that lack import markings or are marked discreetly so as not to affect the pistol's appearance are attractive to collectors and will thus increase value. The possible "mystery" variants identified from images on vz. 70 boxes, one with the vz. 69 safety lever and the other with a flat, horizontally grooved disassembly button, would certainly be interesting if discovered. Values of oddities will depend on their uniqueness, their condition, and the skill of the seller in marketing them. One of the pleasures of studying these pistols has been the discovery of such pieces among the stream of offerings at gun shows and on internet auction sites and the ability to acquire them at modest prices because no one else recognized their uniqueness.

Very early Strakonicé vz. 50s from serial number 650001 through about 650500 merit careful marketing; values will increase with proximity to the serialization starting point. (There are only six pistols from this range recorded in the database, one of them from a private collection in the Czech Republic. Serial number 650564 is the earliest specimen the author has had the opportunity to purchase.) Late Strakonicé pistols with serial numbers above 739000 should also develop increased collector interest if their position in the production sequence is advertised. Early ZUB vz. 50s would be doubly interesting because of their low B-series serial numbers and 57 dates, but there are no records of sales to indicate their value. Vz 70s with serial numbers approaching the 724536 endpoint will also be of interest, but due to their random order of assembly they could be dated 81, 82, or 83; the highest number reportedly used was probably not the last pistol assembled.

Consecutively numbered pairs of pistols are interesting but since vz. 50-70s were completed in random order, the relationship between consecutive serial numbers is merely coincidence. The author acquired vz. 50 serial numbers 664019 and 664020, pictured in chapter 2, in separate sales four years apart because their disparate histories contrasted with their consecutive numbering; he has resisted multiple opportunities to purchase vz. 70s that would have paired with pistols already in his collection because the cost of their acquisition would not have benefited his research. Assuming that both pistols were in very good or better condition, a consecutive pair would probably bring 10–20 percent more than the same pistols offered separately, but marketing is a key factor in justifying their value and the cost of a double purchase could significantly reduce the number of potential bidders. Finding three or more consecutive numbers in decent condition would be much more difficult, but whether it would generate a corresponding increase in interest—and value—is questionable. A consecutively numbered pair from the 1970 transition period, one marked vz. 50 and the other vz. 70, would certainly be interesting but their value would be heavily influenced by condition.

Spare magazines, once quite common, are becoming more difficult to find and prices have risen accordingly. Types 1 through 3, made for the vz. 50 with the early type of finger rest, are much

Chapter 9

more difficult to find than vz. 70 types 4 and 5 and typically sell for $75 or more, depending on condition; types 4 and 5 are generally priced in the $50–$75 range. The type 2 is the least common and should merit a collector premium, but lack of knowledge would make this difficult to realize. Compact types 1a, 2a, and 3a plain-base magazines are more variable in price, ranging from about $45 to $75; a type 5a might bring a premium if properly marketed but it could be difficult to find collectors willing to pay it. After-market replacement magazines are usually offered for $25 to $50, but in the author's opinion they are a poor investment.

Original type 5 holsters have been imported in large quantities, often in unissued condition, and while prices have begun to increase, they can usually be found for $25–$50 on the internet. Early specimens without reinforced closure flaps are usually unmarked but are correct for C- and D-series vz. 50s and all vz. 70s; they are harder to find than later holsters but this is not generally reflected in pricing. The dress versions of this holster are usually offered at about half the price of the standard version, probably because there is little demand for them and, as noted in chapter 8, they may be useless except for display. Types 1, 3, and 4 holsters are difficult to find—the author purchased most of his specimens from European sources—and prices typically run from $50 to $100. Transitional holsters have rarely been imported into the US except as individual specimens mistaken for wartime ČZ 27 holsters; the author's specimens came from a large military warehouse in Artemovsk, Ukraine, and were probably supplied with the 7,000 vz. 50s sold to the Soviet Union in 1950; they have been advertised on the internet for about $50, but the supply appears to have been exhausted. (Unmarked vz. 50 holsters are often erroneously marketed as World War II ČZ 27 holsters at prices of $100–$200; this is probably the result of seller ignorance rather than avarice.)

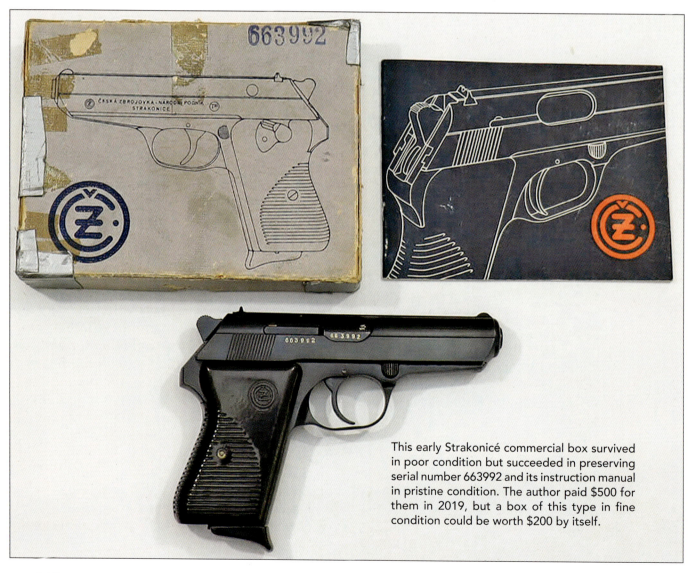

This early Strakonicé commercial box survived in poor condition but succeeded in preserving serial number 663992 and its instruction manual in pristine condition. The author paid $500 for them in 2019, but a box of this type in fine condition could be worth $200 by itself.

142   The ČZ Models 50 and 70

The author has never seen a type 2 holster offered for sale; the specimen pictured was purchased from Europe in an arranged sale for over $400. The vz. 62 holster and its shoulder variant are scarce and are not known to have been imported into the US; the author's specimens were purchased from an eBay.com seller in the Czech Republic for $25 each. Leather StB shoulder holsters are often provided free with vz. 50-70s offered for sale on the internet; individual specimens have been offered for prices ranging from $15 to $50, but fair market value is about $20. The StB belt holster has not been imported in significant quantities but occasionally appears on eBay.com; the author's specimens were acquired from the Czech Republic for $10 each. The associated spare-magazine pouches are occasionally seen at prices of $15 to $25. Bulgarian and East German Makarov holsters will fit the vz. 50-70 and sometimes accompany Czech pistols offered for sale; no holsters of that type were made in Czechoslovakia. The South African vz. 50-70 holsters pictured in chapter 8 are not rare but they have not been widely marketed in the US and are thus difficult to find here. The author's specimens were purchased from South African sellers on eBay for about $30 each plus international shipping; other observed offerings have been in the $40–$50 range.

The survival rate of original cardboard pistol boxes is unknown; private purchasers of the pistols often retain the boxes either for storage or as original accessories, but police departments and other government agencies that bought vz. 50-70s in quantity usually discarded the boxes simply because they required a good deal of storage space and at the time they were issued, eventual resale of the pistols was not a consideration. Surplus dealers sometimes acquire small lots of them and they appear from time to time on internet auction sites. The author did not begin collecting data on vz. 50-70 boxes until well after he began building his database so box records are relatively scarce, but enough is known about them to estimate their numbers and periods of use with reasonable accuracy. Approximately 420,000 of the 1968 vz. 50 boxes were produced, issued from early 1968 through April 1971 and December 1971 through January 1975. Approximately 50,000 early vz. 70 boxes were produced, issued from April through December 1971 and November or December 1974 through January 1975. Approximately 524,000 late vz. 70 boxes were produced, issued from November or December 1974 through the end of production in 1983. Dates on test targets issued with the pistols typically lag behind the pistol's acceptance date; this is noticeable only with pistols accepted near the end of a calendar year, but in the group of boxes listed in table 8-1 many of the targets are undated, probably because they were shot in January 1975 before the new date stamps for that year were available. Individual 1968 vz. 50 boxes with vz. 50 serial numbers are seldom offered for sale but may

Vz. 70 serial number J08375 was produced in April 1971 and was packed in an early vz. 70 box with a scarce white-bordered top; it was imported to West Germany by Waffen Frankonia Würzberg and remained there for forty-one years, evidently being used for target practice but rarely if ever carried. In 2012, it was imported to the US by Heritage Arms of Naples, Florida, and was purchased by the author for $205; unfortunately, its test target was lost along the way. Its 2022 value would be $450–$500.

bring prices of $50 to $100, depending on condition. Those issued with vz. 70s are more common but may still bring as much as $50. Early vz. 70 boxes are also uncommon and may bring prices similar to vz. 50 boxes; the author has seen only three early boxes with a white outline on the top, all with relatively early J-series pistols, but there are not enough data to estimate their actual numbers. Late vz. 70 boxes are more commonly seen and are usually offered for $25–$35. The gray Strakonicé commercial vz. 50 box is rare; the author has encountered only one specimen in nearly twenty years of research and purchased it with its original pistol for a buy-it-now price of $500. Vz. 70s have been offered with plain gray boxes that may have been issued with pistols purchased by the Czech government, but the author has been unable to obtain one for authentication. The boxes' internal liners are fragile and easily damaged by shifting of the pistol during handling and storage; padding the underside of the liner with Styrofoam or cardboard spacers cut to match the pistol's outline will help preserve it. Original cleaning brushes are occasionally included with pistol boxes offered for sale, but they are unlikely to be sold separately because without an associated box or pistol to provide context, very few people would be able to identify them. An included brush should add $10–$15 to the value of a box.

Original manuals and sales pamphlets are difficult to find because few of the pistols were originally marketed in the US; most of the examples shown in chapter 8 came from boxes of miscellaneous firearms publications displayed at gun shows and were purchased for $20 to $35. They occasionally appear on internet auction sites such as eBay.com. As interest in Cold War arms, equipment, and related material increases, values of these items should also increase.

Spare parts for these pistols are often available from internet auction sites or major firearms parts dealers such as GunParts.com and ApexGunParts.com. However, frequently lost or broken parts such as trigger springs and safety detents are often sold out and usually can be obtained only by purchasing a "parts gun" in poor condition or a "parts kit" from a pistol confiscated and decommissioned by a law enforcement agency. Prices on these kits are variable, but they generally sell at auction for $75–$125. There is little interest in serialized parts—stripped receivers, slides, and sideplates—because of the difficulty and cost of obtaining parts to rebuild them. (Sideplates usually require hand-fitting; it may be necessary to try several of them in order to find one that can be mated with a specific receiver and slide.)

Although collectors prefer unaltered original specimens, rare variants occasionally turn up with extensive finish wear but no major damage, making them candidates for restoration. Such work should be done only by a gunsmith with a "track record" of restoration and an understanding of the need to preserve original markings and minimize polishing. Pistols with heavy surface pitting usually cannot be restored without compromising markings and other detail, so such efforts are unlikely to improve their values. Those considering restoration should study original pistols in fine condition, noting areas that are polished such as sidle flats on slides, and those such as sighting ribs and rounded areas on slides that normally retain tool marks. Avoid polishing that rounds corners and edges that are normally left "sharp." As a matter of integrity, restored pistols should always be labeled as such when being offered for sale; experienced collectors can usually spot the evidence of restoration and "faking" a pistol's condition can damage the seller's reputation and may have legal consequences.

New, unserialized fifth-variation vz. 50 slide. A few of these were provided to repair workshops for use on damaged pistols, but they are very scarce today; value could be as high as $200 if properly marketed.

Valuation

Communist-era Czech police equipment, credentials, uniforms, badges, decorations, and related items such as those pictured in chapter 8 appear fairly regularly on eBay.com and other websites specializing in militaria. Pricing is somewhat random and actual value should be determined by someone with a specialized background in Czech military and police history. Cased decorations with documentation are obviously more valuable than similar "loose" material, but both buyers and sellers may need to negotiate to arrive at a suitable price. The author paid $15 to $45 for the items pictured but international shipping costs sometimes exceeded the price of the item.

An appendix is provided below listing the known variations of the vz. 50-70 and their numbers occurring in the database. Its purpose is to provide both buyers and sellers with a tool for assessing the relative scarcity *in the US* of any specimen as a component of its value. The numbers of complementary variants (such as marking variations) will not always add up to the table totals because some records are incomplete, such as a stripped twenty-one-groove vz. 50 slide which offers no data on its hammer type for the database.

1967 vz. 50 serial number C18630, professionally restored by gunsmith Jack Love and fitted with Klinsky walnut grips, is an attractive personal defense weapon but lacks the collector appeal of originality.

Czech Cold War Police Pistols

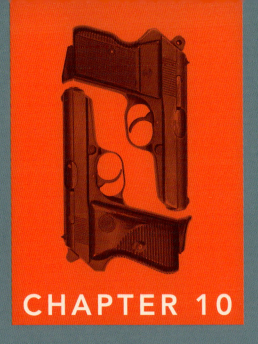

CHAPTER 10

Shooting and Maintenance

Vz. 50-70s are no-frills service pistols and are generally reliable and trouble-free; when problems arise, they are usually caused by damaged magazines. They function well with standard 7.65 mm Browning (.32 ACP) ammunition loaded with 70-to-75-grain FMJ bullets at velocities of 900–950 feet per second (f/s); Czech sources list the Sellier & Bellot loading with a 72-grain bullet at 951 f/s and US commercial FMJ ammunition has similar ballistics. Some high-performance commercial loadings with bullet weights of 55–60 grains advertise velocities as high as 1,050 f/s. The *Hornady Handbook of Cartridge Reloading*, tenth edition, page 852, lists a number of loads with 60-grain bullets at velocities up to 1,000 f/s, while *Speer Reloading Manual # 14*, page 826, lists loads with 60-grain bullets with velocities up to 1,060 f/s. Earlier manuals (e.g., Hornady's *Eighth Edition*) list loads for 71-grain bullets at velocities up to 900 f/s. (NEVER hand-load ammunition that is not based on data published in a reliable loading manual; some internet websites offer reloading data, but it should be used only if the source can be verified as a reliable authority. Approach maximum loads with caution, following manual directions; the use of impact-resistant eyewear and hearing protection when shooting is recommended.) Pistols designed for FMJ ammunition may not feed other types of bullets reliably, so ammunition with hollow-point or unusually shaped bullets should be test-fired for proper functioning in your pistol before relying on them for defensive use.

ČZ 83 hammer spring and improvised spacer installed in the author's "hybrid" test pistol, with vz. 50-70 (*left*) and CZ 83 springs shown for comparison. Note difference between grip tang contours in the pistol's 1950 receiver and 1981 sideplate.

The vz. 50-70 design is inherently accurate due to its fixed barrel and close receiver/slide tolerances, although its 105-degree grip angle may induce the shooter to point low before aligning the sights; the revised vz. 70 grip panel contours offer some improvement in pointing quality over the original vz. 50 design. The 5-inch sighting radius makes precision shooting difficult, especially when coupled with a stiff trigger, but when fired single-action from a rest, vz. 50-70s should group within 3 inches at a range of 25 m.

The double-action trigger pull is unusually stiff due to the hammer spring strength, the lack of mechanical advantage in the trigger linkage, and the added burden of raising the firing-pin lock against its spring. Early vz. 50s generally have trigger pull weights of 13–16 pounds, but hammer spring strength was increased due to problems with the firing mechanism when production was restarted at ZUB, resulting in 18–22-pound trigger pulls that can be difficult to manage. The pull weight can be reduced by cutting two to four coils from one end of the hammer spring, but this should be done cautiously because removing too much length can produce unreliable primer ignition, especially in the double-action mode; it is wise to have a spare spring on hand before making modifications. In the author's testing with modified springs, the double-action pull had to be at least 14 pounds for reliable ignition, although weights as low as 12 pounds fired primers in the single-action mode. Another solution to the pull weight problem is replacing the hammer spring with a stock ČZ 83 pistol spring, together with a 0.010" spacer to compensate for the ČZ 83 spring's shorter length, for a 14-pound pull. (The author used a Crown Bolt #6-32 brass machine nut drilled out to ⅛" for a spacer on his "shooter," which may look like hillbilly engineering but works well.) The ČZ 83 spring is larger in diameter than the corresponding spring recess in the vz. 59-70 hammer spring retainer, making installation more difficult, but it can be readily accomplished with the modified locking-jaw pliers described in chapter 7. Trigger pull can also be improved by replacing the firing pin and its lock with a Harrington Products #CZ50/70-2 competition firing pin and trigger enhancement kit, but this deactivates the firing-pin lock, one of the pistol's safety features, and may allow it to fire when the decocking mechanism is activated.

Dropping a vz. 50-70 with the slide removed can twist the barrel housing enough to alter the pistol's point of aim without preventing barrel/slide alignment; such a pistol will produce shot groups that are consistent but out of alignment with the sight picture. If drifting the rear sight in its notch does not correct this, it can be remedied by clamping the pistol's receiver in a padded vise and using a steel rod inserted in the barrel to realign the barrel housing, but this is a job best handled by an experienced gunsmith; repeated adjustments can produce metal fatigue and weaken the receiver. Other damage to major parts, such as a bent trigger guard or twisted receiver, will require heating the affected area and reshaping it, which should be done only by a competent gunsmith; this will usually also require refinishing the pistol and the repair may cost more than the pistol is worth—ask for an estimate before proceeding with the work. A cracked receiver or slide is usually impractical, if not impossible, to repair.

The firing-pin design used on these pistols is flawed in that, when the pistol is dry-fired, its forward shoulder strikes the inner face of its recess sharply (if a cartridge is chambered, the primer buffers the firing pin's impact, preventing damage). This impact, combined with the firing pin's inertia, produces metal fatigue that eventually causes the tip to break off; dry firing should be avoided unless a snap cap is used. The author has not engaged in destructive testing to determine how many dry-firing impacts are required to break the average firing pin, but the answer would be meaningless to purchasers of used pistols since there is no way to know how many times they have already been dry-fired. The Harrington Products replacement kit noted above eliminates firing-pin breakage; a skilled machinist can lathe-turn a firing pin to set the forward shoulder back as much as 4 mm, replacing the metal removed with a coil spring to absorb impact, but this reduces the firing pin's weight and striking inertia and some "tuning" may be required to ensure that the modification works properly. Replacing the hammer spring to reduce power will also reduce firing-pin breakage but this can affect primer ignition, as noted above. Having one or two replacement firing pins in your spare-parts box is a good investment. The firing pin operates through inertia, its rear breaking contact with the hammer before its front reaches the cartridge primer, and when the recoiling

Chapter 10

slide is stopped after firing the firing pin's rearward inertia moves it back to its locked position. If congealed oil and fouling build up around the firing pin and it is dry-fired, there is no recoil setback; the firing-pin lock spring may be unable to cam the firing pin back to its locked position and the pin may stick far enough forward in its tunnel to be out of reach of the hammer, preventing the pistol from firing until the pin is removed and cleaned. The longer the pin remains stuck in this position, the more the fouling can harden, cementing the pin in place. It is theoretically possible for the pin to become frozen far enough forward to produce a slam fire when a cartridge is chambered, so it is prudent to dismount the firing pin and its lock from any newly acquired pistol and clean the recess and associated parts as described in chapter 7 before use. When at rest, the rear of the firing pin should protrude about 2 mm from the rear of its tunnel into the hammer slot in the rear of the slide, although its domed rear makes this difficult to measure. If it does not protrude into the hammer slot, dismount and clean it and its tunnel before use.

Grip screws should be tightened enough to ensure a snug fit, but overtightening can distort the grip panels and bind the magazine. If this problem occurs, use a flat file to remove a little material from the inside surfaces of the grip panels that face the magazine until the binding is eliminated. Distortion or burring of the locking notch in the magazine body can also cause it to bind in the magazine well, but this is uncommon; look for a protrusion or bright spot around the edges of the notch and use a jeweler's file or emery board to smooth it until the problem is corrected.

The pistol's decocking mechanism was designed to safely lower the hammer over a loaded chamber without firing a chambered cartridge; its operation is discussed in chapter 6. Activating it should be done only with the pistol pointed in a safe direction, since even "foolproof" mechanical devices *can* fail. A vz. 50-70 should be subjected to two safety checks before its first use—and periodically rechecking it is prudent if it is used extensively—always performed with the pistol unloaded. First, with the hammer uncocked and the safety in the "fire" position, attempt to push the hammer forward with the thumb; it should stop after about 2 mm of travel without contacting the rear of the firing pin. This confirms interception of the hammer's safety step by the spur

of the sear. Second, with the hammer cocked and the safety in the "safe" position, insert a 6" length of ¼" dowel into the muzzle until it contacts the breech face. With the pistol pointed in a safe direction, tip the muzzle up and press the safety lever down to activate the decocking mechanism; the hammer should drop without moving the dowel. Recock the hammer, move the safety to the "fire" position, and pull the trigger; the dowel should be launched from the barrel, confirming that the firing pin is intact and the decocking mechanism is working properly. If the pistol fails either of these checks, do not load or attempt to fire it until it has been disassembled and the cause of the failure has been identified and corrected.

It is possible to deactivate the decocking mechanism by filing off a 3 mm section from the left side of the sear spur, preventing the shoulder of the safety from contacting the spur and releasing the hammer when the safety lever is pressed downward from its "safe" position. If a mechanical grinding tool is used, care must be taken to avoid heating the sear enough to lose its tempering. This is not a recommended practice, since manually decocking the altered pistol can lead to an unintentional firing, but it can be done if the owner finds the decocking mechanism to be objectionable.

The clearance between the inside of the slide and the outside of the chamber on the vz. 50-70 is close; as a result, the slide often scratches the right side of the chamber around the serial number during cycling. This does not impair operation, but it can produce undesirable cosmetic damage to the finish. Inspect the inside edges of the ejection port in the slide for burrs or roughness and smooth them with a jeweler's file if necessary; coating the outside of the chamber with a light film of oil will also reduce scratching. If desired, scratches can be touched up with Brownells Oxpho-blue creme.

Each time the slide closes forcefully, it peens the rear face of the chamber; this is more pronounced when it is released on an empty chamber because there is no cartridge in its path to reduce the impact. Over time, this will produce a raised lip around the upper chamber face and while this rarely causes problems, it can eventually cause the slide to drag and affect cartridge chambering. If this occurs, smooth the lip with a jeweler's file, touch up the treated area with Oxpho-blue, and the problem is solved.

The fit between the magazine body and follower is fairly tight; powder residue tends to collect on both surfaces, producing friction that can prevent the follower from moving freely, resulting in failure to feed. Disassembling the magazine and cleaning the follower and the inside of the body with nitro powder solvent and a bore brush will solve the problem; after cleaning, make sure the parts are completely dry before reassembly. Never oil the inside of a magazine, since even small amounts of oil can penetrate and deactivate primers. If desired, use a small amount of dry powdered-graphite lubricant on the inside of the body. Any dents in the sides of the magazine body can impair function and should be removed by inserting a suitable flat mandrel into the body from the bottom and hammering them smooth. Significant dents in the front of the body are more difficult to remove and will require reshaping with a hammer and 0.35" diameter round steel mandrel. Distortion or other damage to the magazine feed lips can also cause feeding problems; reshaping them can be done with a hammer and a jeweler's anvil or the round mandrel noted above, but this may require assistance from a gunsmith. Feeding problems can also be caused by unusually deep tool marks on the feed ramp that are perpendicular to the direction of travel of the bullet during feeding, causing excessive friction; this can be remedied by polishing the feed ramp until smooth.

The hold-open catch on the vz. 50-70 should fit snugly enough to prevent lateral movement, but wear or an inadequately tightened hinge pin may allow the rear of the catch to shift far enough to the left when the slide is removed to snap downward outside the receiver rail where it normally rests. A slightly loose catch will not affect the normal operation of the pistol, but it can block the slide from being reinstalled on the receiver and since it is covered by the slide when this happens, it can be frustrating and rather difficult to identify the problem. Correctly positioning it on top of the rail before mounting the slide will fix the problem temporarily, but it will be necessary to tighten the hinge pin to prevent future problems. If a loose pin allows significant lateral play in the catch, its spring may slip out of its recess when the slide is removed and become lost; the catch will not release normally without the spring, leaving the slide locked in its rear position, which is again difficult to diagnose because the cause is hidden by the slide. Wear on the tip of the

magazine contact spur on early-type catches can prevent them from functioning properly when the magazine is empty; if the slide fails to hold open over an empty magazine, replacement of the catch is usually necessary. A worn hold-open catch spur can also slip under the edge of the magazine follower, preventing the magazine from being removed; when the magazine catch is depressed, the magazine will drop about 1/8" and stop, resisting efforts to withdraw it. If this happens, do not attempt to pry the magazine out, possibly damaging its finger rest; dismount the slide and use a punch or screwdriver to push the follower down past the hold-open catch spur, and the magazine can be removed normally. To prevent recurrence, replace the catch.

Any newly acquired pistol should have its bore cleaned and inspected before firing. After firing, clean the bore with nitro powder solvent and a .32-caliber bronze brush, followed by a dry patch to remove any loose residue and a second lightly oiled patch for protection. Surplus pistols and even factory-new ones often have internal parts coated with protective oil or grease that should be removed before firing; if disassembly is impractical, field-strip the pistol, soak the slide and receiver assemblies in a degreasing solvent, and let them drain thoroughly before reassembly. The recesses for the firing pin and its lock are prone to trap and retain fluids, so it is best to dismount these parts and clean their recesses, as described in chapter 7.

Corrosive-primed ammunition should be avoided, but if it is used, the bore must be promptly cleaned with warm soapy water or an ammonia solution, dried thoroughly, and recleaned with a brush and light oil. The inside of the slide should be wiped with a moist cloth, dried, and lightly oiled. If a vz. 50-70 is immersed in water or subjected to enough wet weather to affect internal parts, the firing pin and its lock and the extractor and associated parts should be removed, their recesses carefully cleaned and dried, and the parts dried before reassembly. The magazine and firing mechanism should also be cleaned and dried, although removing the grip panels, spraying the interior of the receiver with WD-40, and allowing it to drain thoroughly may be sufficient if disassembly is impractical. In the humid South where the author resides, a light film of a protective oil such as Break-Free CLP on internal parts helps prevent rust, although some firearms specialists recommend that

Chapter 10

internal parts be left dry and that is the best policy in a more arid climate, where oil tends to accumulate dust. Light lubrication of the slide-receiver contact points helps ensure smooth operation.

Pistols are occasionally found with "tight" magazine catches, making magazine removal difficult, especially if the pistol is equipped with a magazine-retaining spring. Using a jeweler's file to slightly enlarge the upper front corner of the locking notch on the magazine will solve this problem, but only if that magazine is used in the pistol. To make the pistol accept and release all magazines more easily requires filing the contact surface of the magazine catch itself, which can be done only after dismounting the hammer spring retainer and removing the sideplate.

Because most 7.65 mm Browning ammunition produced after the 1950s uses noncorrosive priming and the cartridge does not generate enough pressure or powder gas volume to cause significant bore erosion, finding a vz. 50-70 with a badly worn bore is unusual. However, visually inspecting the bore and checking muzzle wear with a .308" bore gauge before making a purchase are advisable; a reading of 2 on the gauge is expected and anything above 3 indicates excessive wear. Wear on a pistol's exterior finish is usually a function of the "carry" time it has experienced and the type of holster used, and may be unrelated to internal condition. A good indicator of the amount of actual firing a vz. 50-70 has been subjected to is the impact print of the hold-open catch on the left side of the breech face. To judge this, remove the slide and use a 5× lens and bright light to examine the breech area from the bottom of the slide. Lightly used pistols will show a bright spot where the hold-open catch has begun to peen the breech face; as the amount of use increases, the peened area will develop into a curved indentation pointing roughly toward the firing-pin hole, which may produce enough edge cratering to affect cartridge chambering. (In pistols with the revised hold-open catch, the impact area will be confined to the outside of the cartridge head recess because of the modified shape of the catch, although metal displaced by heavy peening may intrude into the recess.) When vz. 50-70s are fired, they will also develop metal displacement on the bottom of the slide behind the firing-pin lock. The hammer snaps upward after the lock passes over it as the slide returns to battery, producing an indentation; this effect increases with use and is a good indicator of general wear. This type of breech face and slide wear rarely renders a pistol unserviceable and it can be dressed with a Dremel rotary tool if desired, but it reflects corresponding wear on other internal parts that may necessitate future repairs and should be considered when assessing a pistol's value.

The front of the slide has a lug machined into its lower inside face that is 3 mm square and 5 mm long, projecting rearward. It stops the slide during recoil when it contacts the front face of the disassembly button, which has a recess that aligns with the lug when the button is fully depressed, allowing the slide to be drawn far enough to the rear to disengage it from the receiver. With extensive use, the base of the lug

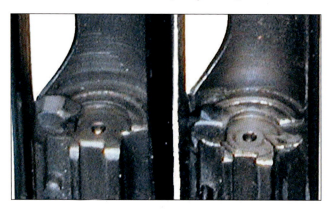

Slide breech faces. *Left*, nearly new pistol with no visible wear; *right*, heavily used pistol with hold-open catch impact print

Bottom rear of three slides, showing peening behind the firing-pin lock. *From left*: light, moderate, and heavy wear.

Bottom front of two slides. *Left*, normal lug; *right*, lug sheared off.

Shooting and Maintenance

Vz. 50 with sideplate removed, showing hooked end of trigger spring pinched between the trigger bar and rear of trigger body, preventing double-action firing. *Below,* the same trigger bar notched to avoid pinching (*top*), and a new, unmodified trigger bar.

develops metal fatigue and may shear off, allowing the slide to overtravel and possibly disengage when the pistol is fired. Any vz. 50-70 with signs of extensive wear should be checked for this defect and considered unserviceable if the lug is cracked or missing. The slide can be replaced, but since new, unnumbered slides are nearly impossible to find, the result will be a mismatched pistol—fine for a "shooter," but devoid of collector value. An expert welder might be able to rebuild a broken lug, but the author has never seen it done.

Another problem that occasionally appears is usually the result of improper installation of the trigger spring, although it can also be caused by substitution of a vz. 52 army pistol spring, with a longer hooked end, for the original. When the trigger is pulled, the hooked end of the spring becomes trapped between the rear of the trigger body and the trigger bar, preventing the firing cycle from being completed. If the problem is an improperly installed vz. 50-70 spring, the solution is obvious. However, if the pistol is equipped with a vz. 52 trigger spring and no correct replacement is available, mark the point on the trigger bar where the spring is being pinched. Remove the trigger bar and file a notch 2 mm deep and 4–5 mm long in its bottom, centered on the pinch mark. This will allow the firing mechanism to cycle properly, providing room for the hooked end of the spring to slide back and forth freely on the trigger bar as the mechanism cycles, and avoiding being pinched.

Binding of the firing mechanism should not develop spontaneously unless a part breaks or dust, pocket lint, or other foreign matter combined with dried grease or oil accumulates to the point where parts cannot move freely. However, a newly acquired pistol may have hidden defects that can cause binding. The first step in solving this problem is to loosen the hammer pivot nut, since overtightening it is the most common source of trouble. If this, combined with judicious application of light oil, doesn't solve the problem, it will be necessary to disassemble the firing mechanism, clean and inspect the parts, and determine the source of the trouble. Use a straightedge on the outside face of the sideplate to see if it is warped from an overtightened hammer pivot nut; straightening it may require the assistance of a gunsmith. Check the inside bearing surfaces on the sideplate and corresponding areas on the trigger bar and other moving parts for burrs or other obstacles to free movement and if necessary, polish any potential problem areas. Replace broken or badly worn parts but if no damage is evident, replacing parts is usually a waste of money—if they worked properly when the pistol was new, a little wear will polish bearing surfaces and should improve operation, not impair it. Springs are an exception to this principle, since repeated flexing produces metal fatigue and eventual breakage, but a broken spring should be easy to identify and replace.

A Bore Stores P-2 case is a good choice for protecting vz. 50-70s and similar-sized pistols.

Czech Cold War Police Pistols 151

Bore Stores (borestores.com) produces silicone-treated polypropylene cloth storage cases with Velcro closures, available from their own website and through a number of retail and internet outlets. Their P-2 small frame case for pistols and revolvers accommodates the vz. 50-70 comfortably, providing rust resistance and padding for protection from mechanical damage. When camping or boating where exposure to water is likely, overwrapping the case with a 1-gallon resealable plastic bag is advisable; add a few dozen Styrofoam peanuts and the bag will float if accidentally dropped overboard. Long-term storage is best done in a climate-controlled space, avoiding moisture and high temperatures.

Replacement magazines are currently produced in the US by Triple K Manufacturing Co.; these magazines are often supplied with surplus vz. 50-70s offered for sale. The body is blued, formed from 0.025" thick steel with a welded rear seam, and has six cartridge-counter holes on each side and a plastic finger-rest floor plate retained by an interior bottom plate that engages a hole in the floor plate's center. The follower is formed from 0.050" steel with downward extensions at the front and rear; the spring is formed from 0.034" steel wire and is 6⅛" long. The author's samples appeared to be of good quality, although less robust than original ČZ magazines, and they fed cartridges reliably but they did not operate the hold-open catch properly when empty. The follower is smaller and not as well supported as the originals, allowing its front to tip downward under pressure from the hold-open catch spring, so the slide is not properly locked open. In the author's tests, the slide usually remained open after the last shot but returned to battery when the magazine was removed.

Pro-Mag Industries produced (but does not currently list) a "CZ-50/70" ten-round extended magazine that typically sells for about $40. It is 5 inches long, is made of steel with a plastic grip spacer and base plate, and has five cartridge-counter holes on the left side. The author's sample would not latch in three of the five pistols in which it was tried and in those that accepted it, the fit was loose and the magazine was difficult to remove because the upper edge of the magazine catch recess snagged on the left grip panel. Inserting the first cartridge into the magazine was difficult because the upper loop of the spring protruded slightly to the left and was trapped between the follower and the magazine body, preventing the follower from being depressed. While this problem was easily remedied by pushing the spring back under the follower, it recurred frequently and could become a serious handicap in a tense situation. The magazine fed cartridges when the action was manually cycled, but due to its other problems it was not taken to the range for extensive testing. Its extra length added ¾" to the pistol's grip, impairing its utility as a pocket weapon, and in the author's opinion its deficiencies far outweighed the value of two extra cartridges. This probably explains why it is no longer cataloged by the manufacturer.

Triple K replacement magazine, easily distinguished from originals by the location of cartridge-counter holes and the shape of the finger rest

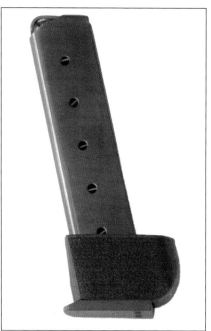

Pro-Mag 10 round extended magazine

MVU Arms replacement magazine finger-rest floor plates

A private individual doing business as MVU Arms produces replacement magazine floor plates that closely resemble the finger-rest floor plates on vz. 70 magazines and are offered for sale on eBay.com. These plates contain no internal metal frame but are made from much-sturdier plastic than the Bakelite used in original finger rests; they fit the magazine bodies well and have a locking slot that interacts with the tip of the magazine spring like the originals. They allow the shooter to easily grasp and remove magazines and are an excellent solution to the problem of missing or damaged magazine finger rests.

Hogue produces universal textured-rubber grip sleeves, the Handall "for most semi-auto pistols" and the Handall Jr. "for most compact autos." The ČZ 50 and 70 are not among the specific models listed for either size, but the author has seen them on vz. 50-70s offered for sale and purchased samples for evaluation. The Handall Jr. is too small for installation; the Handall can be installed, but its bottom must be trimmed to fit the contours of the receiver and grip panels. Whether it is successful or not is a matter of personal preference; it increases the grip's thickness and improves adhesion to the shooter's hand, but as a collector who also shoots these pistols, the author chose not to use it.

Those considering the use of a vz. 50-70 as a defensive arm should be aware of the limitations of the 7.65 mm Browning cartridge. Although widely used outside the US during the twentieth century as a military and police cartridge and dramatized cinematically (the introduction to one James Bond film credits it with "a delivery like a brick through a plate glass window"), it is a marginal defense round. For police use, especially in Europe, a pistol was generally viewed as a weapon to deter or disable rather than kill an opponent, and the 7.65 mm round was generally adequate for that purpose. The cartridge can be deadly with proper shot placement, but it lacks stopping power, especially if your adversary is under the influence of drugs, alcohol, or adrenaline. A 7.65 mm pistol is acceptable for someone who is unable to handle more-powerful weapons, but anyone considering it should take the time to become thoroughly proficient in its use; multiple hits in vital areas may be required to stop a determined aggressor. A moderate amount of hand strength is needed to operate the slide on a vz. 50-70, especially on early variants with fifteen-groove slides, and while this can be ameliorated by the use of leather gloves, you probably won't have time to put them on in a defensive encounter. This should be considered by anyone with arthritis or other limitations to their gripping ability.

Whether you are at the range, in the field, or tinkering with firearms at home or the club, if you are not in a life-and-death defensive situation, *safety must always be your primary focus*. Modern manufacturing components and technology have greatly reduced the probability of misfires and hang-fires caused by faulty ammunition, but such things can still happen and may produce disastrous results; never let your guard down. If you are not familiar with the "Ten Commandments of Firearms Safety," search it on the internet or contact the National Rifle Association. When investigating a firearm's mechanical issues, never use live ammunition; inert dummy or drill rounds or snap caps are the safest option for checking mechanical functioning. Three companies—A-Zoom, Tipton, and Traditions Performance Firearms—currently offer .32 ACP snap caps. A-Zoom caps are precision-machined, anodized red aluminum with synthetic cushion primers; Tipton and Traditions caps are identical except for markings and have clear red plastic bodies with brass case heads and spring-loaded primers, made in Italy. A-Zoom and Tipton caps are available from retail and internet suppliers such as GunBroker.com for $15 to $20 per package of five, while Traditions caps are sold in packages of six for about $25. Saf-T-Trainers makes .32 ACP orange plastic dummy rounds that are less durable but also less expensive than snap caps at $12 per pack of fifty, available on eBay.com; they are also effective for cushioning firing pins during dry firing. The author makes .32 ACP drill rounds by loading a standard FMJ bullet with a 3/32" hole drilled through its center from nose to base into an empty primed case with a 1/8" transverse hole drilled through its body. The holes identify the rounds and allow gas to escape harmlessly when the primers are fired; the hole through the bullet also allows the case to be deprimed with a 1/16" punch and reprimed for use in checking hammer spring and firing-pin function.

Some .32 ACP snap caps and dummy rounds

Appendix
Summary of Variants

This summary tabulates data recorded in the author's database on vz. 50-70 pistols as of November 15, 2022; it is a valid statistical sample of pistols currently in the US, acquired at random over a period of nearly thirty years, and includes 0.40 percent of the total vz. 50-70 production. Its purpose is to provide dealers and collectors with a tool for estimating the relative scarcity of variants they own or wish to acquire or sell in order to establish fair market value. Initially, the database was "frozen" at 1,000 vz. 50s and 2,000 vz. 70s for the utility of those numbers in making mathematical calculations, but this concept was abandoned because vz. 50s from Strakonicé have little in common with those from ZUB in terms of their variations and the manner in which they were distributed; there was also significant information in the records collected since the database was frozen that increases the scope, depth, and utility of the summary. Regarding the relationship between the two models, when the number of vz. 50 records reached the 1,500 mark, the number of vz. 70s stood at 2,500, indicating an approximate 3:5 ratio of vz. 50s to vz. 70s currently in the US.

Readers should note that numbers for some variants are rough estimates, indicated by a following (e), and others are pure guesswork, indicated by a question mark. This is because most records are based on external photographs which do not show internal changes and in some cases there are insufficient data to support a valid estimate. Some photographic records are incomplete because important features are invisible or unclear; due to the missing data, numbers within groups of variants such as marking variations may not equal the table total. Many of the variations overlap, so a single specimen may have multiple attributes worthy of consideration. There is a great deal of variability in the density of the data, with some dates and serial ranges well represented and others quite sparse; this is because some major purchasers of the pistols later sold them on US surplus markets, while others either continue to use them or disposed of them in other ways. Some pistols covered in the text, such as the vz. 69 and Kompaktní, are not included because known specimens are retained in the Czech Republic and the author has been unable to obtain details such as serial numbers and quantities produced. As noted in the preface, the term "unknown" means unknown to the author; there are undoubtedly records in the Czech Republic covering most of this information. In general, "number in the database" figures reflect the relative frequency of occurrence in the US, while "estimated total number" figures reflect factory production, but some estimated totals, such as the "African Contract," are based only on the database because Czech export records are unavailable.

Although the database currently contains records on 0.40 percent of the total vz. 50-70 production, it is divided into three sections. The Strakonicé vz. 50 section contains 939 records drawn from a total of 88,823 pistols, or 1.02 percent. The ZUB vz. 50 section contains 765 records drawn from a total of 268,800 pistols, or 0.28 percent. The ZUB vz. 70 section contains 2,719 records drawn from a total of 745,000 pistols, or 0.36 percent. This means that, proportionately, there is nearly four times as much data on Strakonicé vz. 50s as on ZUB vz. 50s and nearly three times as much as on ZUB vz. 70s. Obviously, the Strakonicé vz. 50 data are the most reliable, and the ZUB vz. 50 data the least reliable but we must work with what we have. The author plans to make periodic updates to this summary, which will be available on request.

The final table of this appendix lists estimated average monthly production for those who wish to approximate the time when a pistol was accepted (e.g., vz. 50 # C83266 was accepted at about the time of the Apollo 11 moon landing, July 20, 1969). Bear in mind that production rates varied within any given year and acceptance was not in serial order, making this a crude tool at best, but it may be interesting to correlate a pistol's acceptance date with historical events, even if the result is imprecise.

Strakonicé vz. 50			
Variant name	**Observed serial range**	**Number in database**	**Estimated total**
First marking	650036–688698	315	30,360
Second marking	664597–714768	313	30,165
Third marking	684344–741045	300	28,298
NB 50	650131–704512	431	34,134
NB 51	679241–720514	146	11,510
NB 52	712419–739535	238	18,356
MS 50	665613–678662	6	500
1950 commercial	650036–690610	49	11,035
1951 commercial	682868–718840	51	11,486
1952 commercial	716656–736392	8	1,802
Weight reduction cut	650036–676273(e)	244(e)	26,237
First slide grip	650036–660000(e)	85(e)	7,530
Second slide grip	660000(e)–730000(e)	733(e)	71,798
Third slide grip	730000(e)–739535(e)	106(e)	9,495
Prototype hammer	(scattered)	9	750
Standard solid hammer	650036–739535	914	88,100
No magazine retainer	650036–739535	28	72,169
Retrofitted retainer	(scattered)	6	16,654
Plum slide	670000–692000	121	11,443
Aluminum grip	659090–659247	3	50–100?
Rebarreled-reproofed	(scattered)	35	3,383
Sport	719608–731571	4	unknown
Factory/shop cutaway	710477–727978, unserialized	4	unknown
dP marked	(scattered)	8	777
50 date	650036–704512	477	45,114
51 date	670617–720514	190	23,195
52 date	712419–739535	246	19,991
Total number of records		939	

Zavod Uherský Brod vz. 50

Variant name	Observed serial range	Number in database	Estimated total
Fourth marking	B10001–D78954	765	268,800
B series	B10001–B99999	230	89,999
C series	C00440–C98453	282	99,999
D series	D07617–D78954	253	78,800
Third slide grip	B10001–C01298	235	89,440
Third slide grip + ring hammer	B99705–C01298	5	5,000?
Fourth slide grip	C01562–C02861	6	1,300?
Fifth slide grip	C03584–D78954	522	175,800
Standard solid hammer	B10001–C18630	222	178,000
Large-hole ring hammer	B99705–D07617	281	108,000
Small-hole ring hammer	D14347–D78954	249	69,000
Smooth machined rib	B10001–B43716	117	33,715
Smooth "forged" rib	B44161–C02861	114	60,297
Impressed pattern rib	C01973–D78944	531	176,971
No mag. retainer	B10001–C04458	237	163,000
Built-in mag. retainer	C05333–D78944	509	173,500
Grooved t-d button	B10001–C98453	478	273,300
Checkered t-d button	C95444–D78944	275	84,300
Smooth trigger	B10001–B21114	31	1,115
Grooved trigger	B18124–D78954	727	267,785
Rebarreled-reproofed	C85482, D68776, D68972	4	unknown
dP marked	C58543	1	unknown
Aluminum grip	D67329	1	50-100?
57 date	B10001–B10510	1	510
58 date	B10347–B25435	61	12,000
59 date	B23437–B31903	23	8,000
60 date	B31710–B323xx	2	2,001
61 date	B33049–B36157	6	4,200
62 date	B36850–B43716	19	7,077
63 date	—	0	171
64 date	B44161–B63797	74	18,800
65 date	B64399–B74344	25	9,944
66 date	B75985–B77514	3	1,529
67 date	B-78260–C20963	54	43,000
68 date	C21714–C69946	143	43,093
69 date	C62779–C98543	69	40,202
70 date	C95444–D78944	251	78,000
Factory/shop cutaway	C20607	2	unknown
Total number of records		765	

Zavod Uherský Brod vz. 70			
Variant name	Observed serial range	Number in database	Estimated total
Vz. 50-70 transitional	D78266–D78512	4	200?
Keyed hammer pivot	D78266–J14191	292	35,792
Slotted hammer pivot	J16538–△723899	2,391	710,336
Original hold-open catch	D78266–278203	1,660	299,803+
Revised hold-open catch	321937–△723899	1,029	412,699+
Sixth slide grip	All vz. 70s	2,719	745,000
Fifth marking	D78266–643200, 708611–722607	1,546	501,141
Sixth marking	△592259–△723899	731	243,859
Star serial prefix	☆352883–☆617981	16	65,000+
D series	D78266–D99919	243	21,200
J series	J00113–J99929	614	99,999
100000 series	100032–199997	590	100,000
200000 series	200041–298624	237	100,000
300000 series	301492–399292	48	100,000
400000 series	401253–487754	35	100,000
500000 series	501310–△597808	55	100,000
600000 series	△601865–△699978	643	100,000
700000 series	△700032–△723899	235	24,536
"African Contract"	J25220–△721778	373	102,239*
70 date	D78266–D86787	73	7,200
71 date	D85357–J91232, 101757–101899	462	85,000
72 date	J60765–162517	611	68,640
73 date	131911–17056x	156	30,806
74 date	164097–203873	189	28,430
75 date	164092–276818	206	60,050
76 date	263887–325726	90	70,440
77 date	278229–431871	58	77,790
78 date	421202–487754	13	66,816
79 date	501310–626832	65	79,837
80 date	☆588598–△654720	131	76,287
81 date	△650819–△723899	727	66,509
82 date	660400–723524	16	8,445
83 date	–	0	425
Factory silencer mod.	D86192	1	110
Factory cutaway	X2001, 10 (SER10DUP import)	2	10?
Total number of records		2,719	
Database total		4,423	

* Probably a gross overestimate due to over representation of "African Contract" vz. 70s in the database

Appendix

Estimated Average Production		
Year	Total production	Monthly average
1950	46,819	4,256 (11 months)
1951	19,055	1,588
1952	22,949	2,550 (9 months)
1957	510	159 (October through December)
1958	12,000	1,000
1959	8,000	667
1960	2,001	167
1961	4,200	350
1962	7,077	590
1963	171	(actual production period unknown)
1964	18,800	1,567
1965	9,944	829
1966	1,592	133
1967	43,000	3,583
1968	43,093	3,591
1969	40,202	3,350
1970	85,200	7,100
1971	85,000	7,083
1972	68,640	5,720
1973	30,806	2,567
1974	28,430	2,369
1975	60,050	5,004
1976	70,440	5,870
1977	77,970	6,498
1978	66,816	5,568
1979	79,837	6,653
1980	76,287	6,357
1981	66,509	5,542
1982	8,445	704
1983	425	(probably less than one month)

Parenthetical notes indicate assumptions used in calculation. It is not known how quickly production reached average output levels after the start-up at Strakonicé, but the number of prototype hammers that had already been fabricated before actual production began suggests that the factory had probably also fabricated other components and was poised for immediate action when the contract was approved.

Bibliography

Dolínek, Vladimír, Vladimír Karlický, and Pavel Vácha. *Czech Firearms and Ammunition*. Translated by Jiří Janda. Prague: Radix, 1995.

Hornady Manufacturing. *Hornady Handbook of Cartridge Reloading, 10th Edition*. Grand Island, NE: Hornady Manufacturing, 2016.

Matyska, Otto. "A VZ70, Especially Designed for Assassinations." *AUTOMAG* 49, no. 12 (March 2012). National Automatic Pistol Collectors Association (www.napca.net), 2012.

Olson, John, comp. *Famous Pistols and Revolvers*. Vol. II. Paramus, NJ: Jolex, 1976.

Pazdera, David. *Legenda jménem CZ / Historie a současnost České Zbrojovky Uherský Brod* [Czech language]. Prague: Mlada fronta, 2016.

Pazdera, David. "Pravní byla Padesatka 55 let pistol z Uherského Brodu." *Střelecká Revue*, January 2013. [Czech language; English translation provided, 2013].

Pazdera, David, and Jan Skramoušký. *Česká zbrojovka / Historie výrobi zbraní v Uherském Brodě* [Czech language]. Uherský Brod, Czech Republic: Česká zbrojovka a.s., 2006.

Skramoušský, Jan, and Vladislav Badalík. *Československé pistole 1918–1985* [Czech language with English and German chapter summaries]. Prague: ARS-ARM, 1996.

Speer Bullets. *Reloading Manual #14*. Lewiston, ID: Speer Bullets, 2007.

Vyskočíl, František, and Jiří Frenzl. *Česká Zbrojovka 60 let České zbrojovky v Uherském Brodě 1936–1996* [Czech language with brief English summary]. Uherský Brod, Czech Republic: Q Studio, 1996.

Index

Abyssinia (*see* Ethiopia)
Accuracy, 147
African Contract, 60, 140, 141
Ammunition, 7.65 mm, 146
Ammunition, corrosive-primed, 72, 73, 149
Anomalies, 64–67, 78
Annual production totals, 17, 24, 36
Assembly, firing mechanism, 102–106

Box, display, 128, 129
Boxes, issue, 122–125, 143, 144
Brush, cleaning, 122

"Carlos the Jackal," 68
Cartridge indicator, 11, 91, 99
China, 72, 73
Cradle, assembly and disassembly, 96
Cut-away pistols, 80–83
Czech proofing law, 13

De-cocking mechanism, 92, 93, 148
Descriptive data, 11
Diagrams, parts, 103
Disassembly, 93–102
Disassembly button, 93, 101, 102

Ethiopia, 12, 60

Firing mechanism, 88–90
Firing pin, 90–92, 98
Firing pin lock, 91, 92, 98, 107, 108

Grip panels, aluminum, 70–73, 136
Grip panels, standard, 42, 47, 71

Hammer (function), 89, 90
History, production, 12–39
Hold-open catch, 51, 52, 149
Holsters, 110–122, 142, 143

Kompactní (compact) pistol, 28, 29, 84
Kratochvíl brothers, 8, 11, 12

Magazine catch, 11, 150
Magazines, original, 48–50
Magazine, Triple K replacement, 152
Manuals, instruction, 126, 127
Markings, grip strap, 12, 13
Merkuria Corporation, 24, 36
Ministry of Defense, 36
Ministry of Foreign Trade (MZO), 12
Ministry of the Interior (MV), 12, 36
Ministry of Justice (MS), 12, 134, 136
Model, plastic, 82, 83

Nomenclature, parts, 102

Přesné Strojírenství, 17
Promotional brochures, 125–127
Proof marks, 13, 58
Property marks, 58–63

Restoration, 136, 145
Retainer, hammer spring, 46, 99, 100
Retainer, magazine, 45, 46

Safety (lever, mechanism), 92, 93
Safety checks, 148
Sbor národní bezpečnosti (SNB), 12, 119, 129–131
Sear, 88–90, 104, 105
Serial numerals, 42, 43
Serial prefix, triangle, 37–38
Serial prefix, star, 36, 135, 136
Serialization, 13, 17, 21
Sights, 11, 79
Silencers, 68, 69
Snap caps, 153
South Africa, 121, 122
Soviet Union, 12, 28
"Sport" pistol, 21, 78–80, 140
Strakonicé (ČZ factory), 12, 17, 21

Tools, disassembly and assembly, 95–97, 99, 101, 104
Tools, pistol, 122
Transitional vz. 70, 29, 73, 74, 139, 140
Trigger, (mechanism), 89, 90, 151
Trigger bar, 88, 89, 151
Trigger pull, 146, 147

Valuation, 132-145
Variations, disassembly button, 45, 46, 84, 87
Variations, encircled caliber, 52
Variations, hammer, 43, 44
Variations, magazine, 48, 49, 50
Variations, magazine follower, 48
Variations, marking, 56–58
Variations, safety lever, 41
Variations, slide grooves, 45, 47
Variations, slide sighting rib, 43
Variations, trigger, 40, 41
Vietnam, Vietnamese, 71–73
Viet Cong, 72
Vz. 69 prototype, 28, 83–85

Waffen Frankonia Würtzberg, 58
Walther PP pistol, 11
Wear, bore, 150
Wear indicators, general, 150

Zavod Uherský Brod (ZUB), 17, 21